THE EVOLUTION OF
A HEEL-GRABBER

A PORTRAIT OF THE PASSIVE-AGGRESSIVE MAN

BOYD & KATHY BARRETT

WINTERSPRING PRESS

COPYRIGHT INFO

CONTENTS

About the Authors

DEDICATION

We would like to dedicate this book to two professional therapists:

Ron Ellington, who helped us navigate some of the troubled waters of our marriage as we began to work out the issues you'll read about in this book.

And Jean Snyder, who in the midst of helping us deal with some recent trauma from physical injury, encouraged us to bring the book out of its 15 year hibernation, because she saw the need for the truths it contains.

INTRODUCTION

Even though the title of this book, *The Evolution of a Heel-Grabber*, was set in stone a long time ago, there have been so many options for subtitles. For reasons that will soon become clear, it could have been *Confessions of a Passive-Aggressive Man*. For a long period of time, it was *A Biblical Picture of the Passive-Aggressive Man* because of the use of a story from the Bible as a template for exploring this often misunderstood topic. We finally settled on *A Portrait of the Passive-Aggressive Man* in order to condense it down to its essence. One option found its way to the lower subtitle on the cover, *How Can Such a Nice Guy Make You Feel So Bad?* While answering that question, this book becomes a brutally honest confession carried along by the deep waters of a biblical narrative.

First of all, we need to get any question about my qualifications to write about this topic out of the way. I've studied the

Bible for most of my life, including university undergraduate and graduate work in religion and biblical languages, and have taught and written about more biblical concepts than I can count. But my greatest qualification is that I am a recovering passive-aggressive myself. I operated with passive-aggressive tendencies for most of my life. How do I know that? My wife told me.

Kathy actually didn't know what it was called, but she knew there was something incredibly wrong with this seemingly nice, kind, gentle man she married. She kept telling me that she couldn't believe anyone could be so mean. She felt like she was being attacked time after time, and she accused me of having the weapon in my hand. I was at a loss to understand what was being revealed about me until I ventured a guess by telling Kathy it might be something called "passive-aggressiveness". Our next visit to a large bookstore found Kathy asking a lady who worked there if there was a book about passive-aggressive men. She apparently asked the right person, because she went straight to a book called "Living with the Passive-Aggressive Man" by Scott Wetzler. As the lady was talking about the book, I walked up behind Kathy just in time to hear, "But there's not much hope for him to change." In spite of that statement, Kathy and I read the book together. It painted the portrait of a passive-aggressive man so clearly that I couldn't help but see the resemblance to my life. We recommend it to anyone dealing with the issues we'll be discussing in this book.

So that was the turning point in the lives of two sadly confused people just trying to understand the cause of the confusion and the pain. Don't misunderstand me. I would have never searched out the answers that have come to us, because I was happy to live my life as it was. But my wife was so focused on understanding the problem and discovering a solution that it left me with a clear choice - join in the search or literally be left behind.

Bluntly put, Kathy forced me to realize that much of my operating system was badly flawed. One of the truths I've learned is that passive-aggressive individuals do not actually know they are operating out of a flawed system. It seems perfectly normal to them - until someone has the strength, patience, and love to show them just how abnormal it really is.

As a follower of Jesus, I find encouragement and direction from the stories of the Bible. I'm sure there are many of you reading right now who do the same. But if you don't share my faith, I encourage you to walk through this book with me to find whatever truths might help you if you find yourself dealing with this issue. My purpose is not to convert you to a particular faith or religion. I believe the truths I found will help anyone who is open to the healing they can bring. Kathy and I have also tried, even though we are husband and wife, to use language that applies also to couples who are not married, such as the term "partner". Relationships between significant others, married or not, can become passive-aggressive battle-fields.

As I was thinking through the story of Scripture to find models for this type of behavior, one character stood head and shoulders above the rest...Jacob, the son of Isaac and the grandson of Abraham. Yes, I'm here to tell you that the third in that well-worn list of patriarchs is a classic case of the passive-aggressive male. His story gives us not only a picture of the problem but also points to the solution. So please let me take you through his story and point out what only two groups of people can see immediately - those who live with passive-aggressive men and the men who are recovering passive-aggressives, like me.

By the way, if you're a male who doesn't know whether you're passive-aggressive or not, ask your partner. If they love you, they'll tell you the truth. Mine did,...which tells me that she loves me. If you're in a relationship and know that something is wrong with your partner's inner workings but don't know what to call it, maybe this will help. If you wonder how such a nice guy can make you feel so bad and so confused, I think I know the answer. He's just got an operating system that's messed up and needs to be replaced. The important thing to remember is that God is great at doing just that. And it's never too late to start the process. I was in my mid-fifties when I began writing this book, and it was only a few years before that when I started seeing this tendency in my life and what it really does to the ones I love. But seeing it is the all-important first step. My prayer for this little study is that it will be used to open the eyes of anyone who needs to take that step. And just like a book was used to open my eyes, this one is designed to open eyes and bring hope.

NOTE: I actually completed the first draft of this book almost fifteen years ago and presented it to Kathy to get her final approval before sending it out into the world. She made some notes concerning places she felt needed changes or further explanation and told me the book wasn't quite ready at that point. I, in typical passive-aggressive fashion, worked on it a bit more and then set it aside for *five years*! At that point, I pulled the manuscript out from under a pile of stuff in my closet and sat down to re-read it. The truths on those set-aside pages hit me again like a ton of bricks, and I'm certain they can bring life and healing into relationships haunted by this dysfunction. So...I went back through the text, made Kathy's changes, and then waited another ten years for a point in my life when I'm willing to endure the baring of my soul that takes place in this book. I've finally reached that point, so I'm now handing it to you. Sorry for the delay. But please understand that this process has been a painful one for both

Kathy and me. As we've gone back through it together fifteen years after the first draft, it has been emotionally devastating to relive the pain that was caused by allowing this dysfunction to have such control over my life. If it were not for the tremendous change we've seen in our lives since that time, sharing it like this would be unthinkable. But...here we go...

In the first chapter, we'll look at the incredible picture the book of Genesis gives us of passive-aggressiveness working in Jacob from the moment he came out of the womb.

1. Dysfunctional from the Womb

As I was first writing this chapter, I was awaiting the "any-day-now" news that our daughter-in-law, Sally, was going into labor. And that labor was set to produce not just one but two babies. That's right. My wife and I are the proud grandparents of twin boys who had just not shown up at that point in time.

I suppose this caused me to think a little more about what it's like for two little guys to be in the same womb. The two we were looking forward to welcoming into our world are fraternal twins, so they were in separate sacks, but we've learned that they could still almost touch each other through the sacks. And I'm sure Sally sometimes felt like Rebekah when she was carrying another set of fraternal twins, Jacob and Esau.

The babies jostled each other within her, and she said, "Why is this happening to me?" So she went to inquire of the Lord. The Lord said to her, "Two nations are in your womb, and two peoples from within you will be separated; one people will be stronger than the other, and the older will serve the younger." When the time came for her to give birth, there were twin boys in her womb. (Genesis 25:22-24)

So Rebekah was feeling the struggle of two nations in her womb - not just two boys, like our daughter-in-law. The implications of that struggle were felt for years between the descendants of Rebekah's boys, but the description of their birth in the next few verses shows that the struggle began with two individuals. And there is an image in that description that perfectly depicts the core modus operandi of the subject of our study, the passive-aggressive man.

The first to come out was red, and his whole body was like a hairy garment; so they named him Esau...After this, his brother came out, with his hand grasping Esau's heel; so he was named Jacob (Genesis 25:25-26)

The first act of Jacob's life was to take hold of the heel of his brother, who was obviously coming out of the womb first. This afforded him a little bit of a free ride, since his brother was paving the way for him. His action was not missed by those at the birth, because he was named Ya'aqob, which means "he who supplants" and comes from the root word 'aqeb, which means "heel". That simple act of grabbing Esau's heel as he entered the world became the picture of how he would deal with people throughout his life.

When I look back at how I've dealt with people in my life, especially my wife, I can see how this picture of a heel-grabber is very appropriate. I've come from behind and seized control of situations by utilizing the energy of the person I want to control. Heel-grabbing is the most creative form of manipulation on the market. This study of Jacob will shed light on the inner workings of a heel-grabber, which is the perfect word-picture to describe the passive-aggressive man.

The story of Jacob grabbing Esau's heel as they exited the womb has haunted me ever since I first discovered its power as an almost flawless metaphor for how I approached relationships for most of my life. That's why the title of this book, *The Evolution of a Heel-Grabber*, is so important to me. What has happened since I allowed myself to face this destructive dysfunction in my life has truly been an evolution. Where I am now is far removed from where I was when Kathy and

I first heard those words from that brutally honest lady in the bookstore, "...there's not much hope for him to change". It has been a long road marked by one small victory after another and splattered with the tears of small defeats along the way as well. The lady was right. There's not *much* hope. But there is hope. My evolution proves it.

Thoughts From Kathy

Look Out Behind You!

"Heel-grabber" really is a good word picture for passive-aggressiveness. There have been many times when it has seemed like Boyd came up from behind and manipulated me when he didn't want to say "no" to something or speak up and give his opinion. He would figure out a way to get me to say what he wanted to say, or he would step back and let me make a decision or take care of something unpleasant to him, like our family's finances. Even though I'm good at planning, decision-making, and even financial administration, it was not healthy that he pushed it all off on me. In other words, he would use my strengths to get what he wanted, so that he could avoid confrontation, consequences, or responsibility. What passive-aggressive people don't understand is that they ultimately give up their own person by doing this.

One of the first things I want to make clear is that a partner of a passive-aggressive man will have at least a hint or maybe even a full recognition whenever the dysfunction is making its way toward them. It is at that point that the partner's heel needs to be pulled away before it can be grabbed. And when the passive-aggressive man tries to minimize the alarms sounding inside his partner, that's the time to stand firm. Hopefully, this book will provide some tools to make that easier.

2. GETTING INSIDE THE TENT

Well, after writing that first chapter on a Saturday night just over fifteen years ago, we were awakened at 2:51 the next morning by a call from our son, Asher. We drove to Albuquerque and spent a long day in the hospital waiting for our two little guys to arrive. They made it into our world Sunday evening at 8:17 and 8:19 PM. I could go on for a long time about the twins in our life, but now we need to get back to the second of those famous biblical twins.

The next stop on our journey through the life of our protagonist is found in the next few verses.

So the boys grew. And Esau was a skillful hunter, a man of the field; but Jacob was a mild man, dwelling in tents. And Isaac loved

Esau because he ate *of his* game, but Rebekah loved Jacob. (Genesis 25:27-28)

The first thing that jumps out at me in this passage is **"Jacob was a mild man, dwelling in tents"**. The typical profile of a passive-aggressive man is one who, according to every outward appearance, is mild-mannered and easy-going. He seems to be the easiest person in the world with whom to have a relationship...unless, of course, you want to have a real relationship, which is impossible with a man **"dwelling in tents"**.

Now, I realize that this passage is talking about Jacob physically dwelling in tents as opposed to his brother being an outdoorsman. And it's clear that passive-aggressive men come in both varieties - the indoors, creative type and the outdoors, physical type. But I believe the "beneath-the-surface" meaning is that Jacob, like most passive-aggressive men, dwelt in tents in an emotional sense. He lived within the tent of his own little universe, which he created through manipulation of others. That "tent" is the same enclosure that passive-aggressive men are often very content to call their home.

These verses also tell us that **"Isaac loved Esau... but Rebekah loved Jacob"**. This obviously reveals some dysfunction within their family, but it's not so unlike the dysfunction in most families. Because every father and mother who has ever attempted to raise children is severely flawed by his or her own faults and fleshly tendencies, it's the rare exception for a child to grow up without being affected adversely by those faults and tendencies.

In this story, the favoritism shown by Rebekah toward Jacob caused him to take on her bent toward manipulation. He learned many of his "behind-the-back" controlling ways by watching her operate. I don't know that Rebekah was a full-fledged passive-aggressive individual, but it is very obvious from the storyline that, after appearing at first to be a very willing, pliable, and "mild" addition to the chosen family, she was willing to do whatever she needed to do to get what she wanted, including deception.

It was Rebekah who encouraged Jacob later in life to deceive his father into giving him the blessing that should have gone to Esau as the firstborn. And when Esau wanted to get revenge by taking Jacob's life, it was Rebekah who encouraged Jacob to flee and covered his tracks by telling Isaac that she would just not be able to live if Jacob took a wife from the women of Canaan. (Genesis 27:46)

It's clear to me that at least part of my own relationship issues stems from patterns I learned from my mother, who probably learned them from one of her parents, who probably learned them from...and it goes on and on. Therefore, I don't blame her for anything. It just helps me to understand the origins.

When I think of my mother, who passed away just a few years after I wrote the first draft of this book, I remember someone who was very mild-mannered and non-confronting. My father, who passed away a good number of years before my mother, was very straightforward. I have a feeling that my mother used some passive-aggressive tactics in her relationship with him.

In fact, a scene from my memory that at first seems pretty innocuous, has come to the surface time after time as a pivotal point in my early years. When I was probably 6 to 8 years old, my mother bought me a subscription to a magazine called *Highlights*. I actually think they still publish that magazine, which is a great source for developing reading and creativity in children. For me to have a subscription was a very big deal in our lower middle class family. When my father got home from his job on the assembly line of a tire manufacturer and found out that my mother had spent the money on the subscription, he was furious, and what ensued was the *only* time I ever saw or heard my parents have a serious argument. And my young mind picked up that it was *about me*.

That scene may have impressed on little Boyd's mind that one way to get something you want is to acquire it behind the back of the person who may be opposed to it. It's the old "easier to ask forgiveness" strategy. A child watching parents navigate life is like being taught an operating system that sticks around, whether welcome or not.

Although discovering the patterns in my mother's life has helped me see my own, I don't want to use any other specific situations in her life as examples. I will open up my own life history instead, because this study centers on the passive-aggressive MAN. And the parallels with the patterns in the life of Jacob are striking.

THOUGHTS FROM KATHY

SMOTHERING SWEETLY

Passive-aggressive women seem extremely sweet. They rarely express their opinions, and they often serve others as a vehicle to get their own way. A mother with this dysfunction has a hard time allowing her children to grow up. She doesn't want her children to express anger or experience the negative emotions that come with learning things the hard way. So she unknowingly passes on to her children her own weakness, and those children often become co-dependent with her in her dysfunction.

We all tend to produce offspring after our own kind, and we all have issues that get passed down. The key for parents who struggle with passive-aggressiveness is to give their children boundaries and freedom within those boundaries to make their own decisions and solve problems on their own, even if that means they have to suffer some negative consequences and express anger in the process. That may be one of the hardest things for a passive-aggressive parent to do, but it is the only way their children can become their own persons.

3. WITHHOLDING

The next scene in our story reveals two of the primary weapons in the passive-aggressive man's arsenal - and believe me, he does have an arsenal.

Once when Jacob was cooling some stew, Esau came in from the open country, famished. He said to Jacob, "Quick, let me have some of that red stew! I'm famished!" Jacob replied, "First sell me your birthright." "Look, I am about to die," Esau said. "What good is the birthright to me?" But Jacob said, "Swear to me first." So he swore an oath to him, selling his birthright to Jacob. Then Jacob gave Esau some bread and some lentil stew. He ate and drank, and then got

up and left. So Esau despised his birthright. (Genesis 25:29-34)

First of all, Jacob withholds from Esau something that his brother needs. Secondly, he does so when Esau is most vulnerable. These are two things that show up time and time again in a passive-aggressive man's dealings with those around him, whether it's his partner, father, mother, child, friend, employer, employee, or co-worker.

Now if Jacob had been a normal brother, he would have freely given Esau the food he needed at the time. But his passive-aggressiveness took over as he watched his brother, who had the lion's share of their father's affection, and who more than likely had bullied his little brother as they grew up, bringing his need into Jacob's sphere of influence. It's clear that Jacob knew exactly what he was doing by withholding the stew at that moment. He wanted something out of the situation, and he was willing to manipulate his brother to get it.

In many if not most situations where passive-aggressive men withhold something needed by other people in order to get something from them or punish them for something they've done, they actually are not aware that they're doing it - unlike Jacob, who was very aware and deliberate. However, that does not make the withholding any less of a weapon. I can tell you from experience that many times it comes as a surprise to the passive-aggressive man when he discovers what he's done. And it's even more of a surprise to the person on the receiving end of the withholding that the man doing this to him or her is not aware of what's he's doing.

This is especially true when the other element comes into play. The timing of the withholding just happens to be when the other person is most vulnerable, like Esau was in his hunger. That makes it very difficult for the other person to not believe that whatever is done or not done is a conscious attack meant for harm.

The fact that the passive-aggressive man may not be aware that he is wielding a weapon is the key barrier that keeps the man and those who love him in the dark regarding the source of his actions. That source can be summed up in one word - anger. This kind of man has not developed an inner system to deal with his own anger - or the anger of anyone else, for that matter. Anger scares him. He is terribly threatened by his perception of what anger does when it's unleashed. That's why he fears self-assertion, which he imagines will lead to unchecked anger. In other words, he becomes the mild-mannered Bruce Banner anticipating in horror becoming the huge green personification of anger known as the Incredible Hulk.

Reading this again made me realize that I reverted completely to third person, talking about the passive-aggressive man but not accepting the blame for misappropriating anger myself. Maybe it's because of how truly scary it is to face down my own Incredible Hulk.

I can remember so many times when that green monster rose up to very near the surface of my emotions, only to be pushed back down, because...well, because who wants the world to see that side of themselves? Definitely not the passive-aggressive man. Whoops! There I go again. Let's try that one more time. Who wants the world to see that side of themselves? Definitely not me.

This fear kept me from expressing healthy anger throughout my life and led me to find other ways to express emotions that might lead to anger. As you will see in the next chapter, withholding is one of the more creative of those ways.

Thoughts From Kathy

Angry Nice Men

When I look around at the men in my world who appear to be passive-aggressive, they actually don't always fit the same mold. Some have a hard time doing what they need to do to meet their full potential. Boyd has struggled with that. But I also know very successful men who show strong passive-aggressive tendencies in their relationships. Another common trait of passive-aggressive men is to consistently be late, which is a form of withholding and control. However, Boyd is very punctual and arrives places early most of the time. So it's hard to pin down a stereotype. The most common thing I hear from the victims of this kind of man is the surprise that aggression or anger of any kind could be the issue, because the guy just seems to be so nice.

4. THE WEAPONS OF THE WITHHOLDER

There are several types of withholding that are seen in the passive-aggressive man. The first is the withholding of information. There are many times when a passive-aggressive man has knowledge at his disposal that would help someone in his life to either understand something or be able to get through a tough situation more easily. In those situations, information withheld can be used to hurt or punish the other person. Hurting or punishing is not always the conscious reason for withholding, but when all is said and done, that is the end result. As long as a man lives in his own little universe, he does not see clearly his own motivations. Everything centers around his own needs, so it's difficult for him to see the harm he does to others.

Example: Quite a few years ago, Kathy and I were going through counseling together. Kathy asked me to tell the counselor about a particular incident that would help him understand some of the issues we were going through. She believed it would be better if the counselor heard this from me, and it would have prepared him for his session with her later. Although I cannot remember consciously thinking that I could hurt Kathy by not telling the counselor, that's exactly what I did. I withheld the information that would have paved the way for a much more effective session for Kathy. I also withheld the information from Kathy so that she went into the session blind, thinking I had done the one thing she had asked me to do. When she realized the counselor obviously didn't know what she was talking about, Kathy knew that I had found a way to come through the back door (heel-grabbing) and punish her for something, possibly for insisting that we get this type of help. I would not have been able to give you a good explanation at the time, because I simply did not know I was being deceptive.

Notice that we now have an additional meaning for the term "heel-grabber". Not only does it refer to latching onto someone else's momentum or emotional energy to achieve an end result, but it is also the best picture (other than "a knife in the back") of coming around behind an unsuspecting person to punish them for something they did or said that remained buried deep in the passive-aggressive man's memory until it dug its way out at an especially vulnerable time. And withholding information can be a devastating version of this kind of punishment.

The second type of withholding is when a man withholds an action that would benefit another person. It doesn't matter whether that action is large or small, because when it is withheld, it causes harm to the other person and to the relationship. Again, this often happens at a point of vulnerability for the other person.

Example: When Kathy's grandmother, who she loved deeply, passed away, one thing that I agreed to do was to make a call to our church and our friends to let them know, so that the typical support process could start. I did not make that call, so that meant that our friends and church family did not show up at the funeral or even have the chance to call and express their concern. When Kathy noticed they were not there, she asked me if I had made the calls. My lame response was, "I forgot." I'm sure that if I dug back deep enough, I would be able to find something in my relationship with Kathy in the days before this happened that would have sparked some anger within me that lay hidden until that vulnerable point in her life when my passive-aggressiveness saw an opening to withhold an action that would make her life easier and provide something she needed. Once again, I was not aware of being devious in that moment, but the harsh truth is that my inability to deal with anger in a proper way caused it to seethe within me until it saw an opportunity to come out and hurt Kathy once again from behind (heel-grabbing).

The third type of withholding involves the passive-aggressive man's biggest fear, sharing emotions. When this type of man holds back from sharing his emotions with someone he loves, it results in an incredibly confusing message. The emotions are actually there, but years of placing them on the back-burner and not allowing the other person to experience them make it look like the passive-aggressive man is emotionless. That is not the case, but it might as well be, because the withholding of emotions, especially in the moment of the other person's vulnerability, is perhaps the most devastating weapon this type of man can deploy.

The examples of this are too numerous to list. Suffice it to say that a passive-aggressive man like myself acutely realizes that the emotions are right there on the surface and would love to be able to express them. However, he knows that not doing so withholds something from the one he loves and yet desires to punish. As weird as that sounds, it is most definitely the case. There are times when the simple withdrawing of the normal day-to-day presence of and communication with the passive-aggressive man is weaponized into a form of punishment. Taking away the typical banter between two people who live together and love one another or drastically reducing the number of calls received from your life partner can be unsettling, and the passive-aggressive man knows that. And that leads to an even deeper and more destructive withholding.

Although the withholding of affection is tied to the withholding of emotions, I think it deserves a category of its own. There may be some passive-aggressive men (or should I say men in general) who simply have problems showing physical affection, but I believe there are many passive-aggressive men who do not share that deficit and yet still use the withholding of affection, especially with their wives, as a way to express an anger not released at the proper time. And then guess who gets the blame for there being a lack of physical intimacy – certainly not the passive-aggressive man.

The bottom line is that the waves of intimacy are incredibly difficult for a passive-aggressive man to navigate. His boat does not have the equipment necessary to stay afloat in those waters, so he quite naturally chooses to stay safely on the shore. To be brutally honest, this has been one of the last wounded places in my relationship with Kathy to experience healing. At least we are now traveling the choppy waters in the same boat.

Intimacy requires open communication, and by undermining the possibilities for this, the passive-aggressive man shuts the door to a true relationship.

Thoughts From Kathy

Whether He Meant To Or Not

It was so damaging to our relationship when I found out from other people about things Boyd either did or withheld from doing that negatively affected me. Even those times when Boyd told me what he had done, it usually was too late to do anything about it.

Boyd's typical response was "I didn't mean to." I eventually had to counter that with "It doesn't matter whether you meant to or not. What you did hurt me (or embarrassed me)." That takes it out of the arena of motives, since a passive-aggressive man often is not in touch with his motives, and centers in on the effects of his actions. He doesn't understand that he really did mean to, so you can't argue with him at that level.

5. THE POSTER BOY OF DECEIT

Before we go any farther recounting Jacob's foibles (and, through extension, mine), we need to stop a moment in the very next chapter of Genesis and see that the seeds of the next passive-aggressive signpost we will explore in Jacob were very much there in the life of his father, Isaac, as well as his grandfather, Abraham. Isaac followed in his father's footsteps by lying to Abimelech and claiming that Rebekah was his sister in order to save his own life (Genesis 26:6-11). Abraham had originated the pattern when he claimed the same thing about Sarah (Genesis 12:10-20).

The bottom line of this pattern is that a lie can be justified in the mind of the person telling the lie if the end result is important enough. For a passive-aggressive man, protecting the little universe in which he lives becomes an important enough end result to justify a number of lies. And, just as is the case with withholding, there are times when the passive-aggressive man deceives himself into seeing a lie as the truth.

Now, Jacob followed the pattern laid down by his father and grandfather and took it a step farther by deceiving that very father. His other role model, Rebekah, provided aid and comfort to the passive-aggressive tendencies that had already been operating in Jacob's life.

The dysfunctional inner workings of this family are seen very clearly in Genesis 27, when Rebekah overheard Isaac telling their elder son, Esau, to go out and hunt some game and bring him some good-tasting food so that he could have a good meal and bless his son before he died. She told Jacob about it and told him to go get the best of their flock of goats so that she could cook some meat that would taste exactly like what Esau would bring to his father. When she revealed that her plan included Jacob taking the meat to his father in order to get Esau's blessing, Jacob reminded his mother about the difference in the amount of hair on the two brothers' bodies. Apparently, Rebekah had already thought of that, because she took the skins from the goats and covered Jacob's hands and neck and sent him in to his father. Although Isaac, who was blind by this time in his life, did have questions about which son was in front of him, Jacob was able to fool his father into giving him the blessing that should have gone to Esau.

Jacob said in verse 12,

> **"Perhaps my father will feel me, and I shall
> seem to be a deceiver to him; and I shall bring
> a curse on myself and not a blessing."**

Did it hit you that Jacob was not concerned that he was being a deceiver but only that he would **"seem to be a deceiver"** to his father? The outward impression somehow becomes more important to a passive-aggressive man than the reality of actions and motives. Jacob also brought God in on the deception when he told Isaac in verse 20 that he was able to kill something and bring it back so quickly **"because the LORD your God brought it to me."** Spiritual language is most definitely in the toolbox of many passive-aggressive men and has been pulled out to cover what is one of the most grievous affronts to spirituality - the bald-faced lie.

This is one of the most difficult revelations a passive-aggressive man has to accept if he is going to have any hope of walking out of this enormously destructive lifestyle. The sad truth is that, even though many times the passive-aggressive man does not actually realize what his motives are, any passive-aggressive man who has a conscience does know when he is lying - but does it anyway. Just like Jacob, he goes into a situation knowing that protecting his universe from being invaded by reality requires deception that many times manifests as an obvious lie.

A simple self-justification can grow into something much larger when the first self-justification (read "lie") has to be defended with another self-justification, etc., etc. It's a common human trait to be able to reduce the distance between the truth and what you have come to believe (cognitive dissonance), but the passive-aggressive man has honed that ability into a fine art.

Well, I just spent a great deal of time explaining (quite well, I thought) how passive-aggressive men walk the fine line between lies and the truth, with their heaviest foot regularly landing on the side of the line populated by lies. However, what I didn't say clearly is that I was, for at least half of our marriage, a liar. Yes, I knew when I was doing it. And yes, I came up with clever self-justifications for each and every one of those lies. This is so toxic that today I can smell it coming from a mile away. If only my sense for the smell of deception had been keener in the first half of my life with Kathy.

THOUGHTS FROM KATHY

SPEAKING THE TRUTH IN LOVE

S peaking reality stirs up anger in a passive-aggressive man more quickly than anything else. Boyd would most of the time be totally unaware he was living in a world of his own making until I spoke the truth as clearly as I could. And it is so important to present a black-and-white case when confronting this kind of behavior. Boyd was very good at getting me off track and onto some side issue, many times turning the focus back on me - the tone of my voice or something I had done or said that was totally unrelated to the situation we were dealing with.

My word to partners of passive-aggressive men: Don't let them do that!

Stick to the facts of a situation and guard yourself from being sucked into their unreal world. If you don't, you can easily get caught up in a vicious cycle that never sees a resolution.

6. THE ROAD TO RESTLESSNESS

I thought the last portion of this painful exposé of passive aggressiveness in men like Jacob and me was pretty tough. And the ease with which we have allowed lies to be part of our story certainly was difficult to swallow. But then I looked at the next part of the story - the part that shows how those lies and all the rest of the passive-aggressive tendencies dramatically affect others.

The 27th chapter of Genesis continues with the inevitable discovery by Isaac that he had been deceived along with Esau's realization that he had been robbed. When Esau came in with the actual meal Isaac had ordered and both father and son realized what had happened, their reactions are pictured in verses 33-34:

> **Then Isaac trembled exceedingly, and said,
> "Who? Where is the one who hunted game
> and brought it to me? I ate all of it before you
> came, and I have blessed him—and indeed
> he shall be blessed." When Esau heard the
> words of his father, he cried with an exceed-
> ingly great and bitter cry, and said to his
> father, "Bless me—me also, O my father!"**

Two phrases in this passage in the NKJV grabbed me by the
neck and began the choking process. When Isaac discovered
that he had been fooled by his younger son into thinking he
was the older son, he **"trembled exceedingly"**. And when
Esau found out, he **"cried with an exceedingly great and
bitter cry"**. **"Exceedingly"** is the key word for me. I have often wondered why Kathy has exhibited very strong emotions
whenever she has been confronted with something I've done
(or not done) that was birthed from passive aggressiveness.
My first thought has always been that she was over-reacting.

Isaac and Esau just jumped off the page of Genesis 27 and became Kathy's staunch defenders. It's as if they've surrounded
me with the horrible truth that the things I've put Kathy
through over the years are truly far worse than I'd ever allowed
myself to admit. Kathy knew it, and that's why she has re-
acted (not over-reacted) the way she has. But until Isaac and
Esau chimed in and provided examples of the gut-wrenching

emotions that come in response to passive-aggressive men, I was still in a state of partial denial.

That denial led me to a place of minimizing the harm I was doing to our relationship. I can remember so many times Kathy telling me that she felt like she was carrying a backpack full of rocks, because each time I did something that damaged our marriage, another rock would be placed in the backpack. Now in my mind, of course, I was not the one inserting the rocks! I pleaded with her to forgive me of all of those "past" issues, by taking off the backpack or at least dumping out all the rocks. I had convinced myself that I would be able to overcome this dysfunction much more easily without that backpack constantly reminding both of us of my past failures.

What I didn't realize was that my past record had forced her to keep that full backpack on when she was dealing with me, because if she let down her guard by forgetting about all those other rocks, she would be blindsided when the next one came hurtling at her. That doesn't mean that she didn't forgive me, though sometimes very slowly, but those rocks in that backpack were important reminders to both of us of how seriously we needed to take the damage this dysfunction was bringing to our lives.

I guess the most positive part of this story for the person affected by the passive-aggressive man is the fact that Isaac prophetically proclaimed in verse 40 that Esau would break Isaac's yoke from his neck.

By your sword you shall live, and you shall serve your brother; and it shall come to pass, when you become restless, that you shall break his yoke from your neck."

Although Jacob did receive through deceit the blessing that belonged to Esau, which meant that Esau would continue to be affected by that deceit for a period of time, Isaac saw that future moment when Esau would break the bonds created by that deceit. It would come when he became "restless".

There came a time in Kathy's life, as happens with many women in relationship with passive-aggressive men, when she grew "restless" regarding how my dysfunction was affecting her. I'm sure it was a moment (or a collection of moments) that drove her past a sand-drawn line and made her stand up to what was a destructive force in our relationship. It was a difficult confrontation, but now I'm glad that "restless" moment came.

THOUGHTS FROM KATHY

GROWING RESTLESS

The "restless" moment for me came when I saw the destructive consequences of Boyd's passive-aggressiveness in our kids. His fear of confrontation caused him to go to two opposite extremes. He would either not allow the kids to grow up by refusing to insist that they take responsibility for themselves, or he would treat them like they were already grown up by allowing them to go out into the world without any boundaries or direction. Whenever I tried to bring some balance to these extremes, I came across as the "bad guy" in the situation, and the kids learned how to use this dysfunctional cycle to their advantage. We all faced some tough times during their teen and early adult years that could have been avoided if we had dealt with the dysfunction earlier.

I also got tired of having the weight of being responsible for our marriage, our children, and our future on my shoulders. So...yes, I grew restless.

7. COMMITTING CONDITIONALLY

The next portion of the Genesis narrative gives more of an insight into Esau than Jacob. It describes his intense anger about his brother's actions and how they turned his life upside down. That anger caused him to plot to kill Jacob (Genesis 27:41) and deliberately go against his father's wishes and take a wife from among **"the daughters of Canaan"** (28:6-9). These are far from exemplary responses, but they are exactly that - responses...responses to the toll his brother's passive-aggressive dysfunction had taken on his life. So, although we cannot excuse Esau for his actions in this family drama, we can certainly look at them with some understanding.

As we follow Jacob's movements in this chapter of his life, we find him taking his mother's advice (of course) and getting the heck out of Dodge before his gunslinger brother has a chance to call him out to the dusty streets of Canaan for a shootout (sorry about the extended metaphor, but I couldn't help myself). Jacob headed for the home of his Uncle Laban, who just happened to have a very pretty daughter. But before we get to the love story part of the narrative, we are told that Jacob spent what would be the first of the two most incredible and life-changing nights of his life.

Chapter 28:10-22 describes Jacob's dream of a ladder reaching to heaven with angels ascending and descending on it and the personalizing to Jacob of the promise God had first given to his grandfather and then to his father. It was an incredible promise of blessing, and when Jacob raised his head up from his stone pillow, he exclaimed in verses 16-17,

> **"Surely the LORD is in this place, and I did not know it." And he was afraid and said, "How awesome is this place! This is none other than the house of God, and this is the gate of heaven!"**

What an experience! Jacob encountered the God known so intimately by his father and grandfather in the form of the pre-incarnate Son, who showed Himself to be the connection between heaven and earth and renewed specifically to Jacob the promises already made to Abraham and Isaac. This could have been the turning point in his life, a turning point which could have allowed God to heal him of his dysfunction. But it was not to be. Although Jacob recognized that he was in a special time and place and proclaimed the awesome presence of God in that place, his passive-aggressive tendencies were still alive and kicking even in such an atmosphere.

He first of all did what any person of that era would have done to commemorate his encounter with God. He set up a pillar or standing stone. But the vow he made in connection with the dedication of Bethel was a contingent one. Instead of simply accepting God at His word with all the attending promises, Jacob felt the need to put a contingent clause on his obedience. In verses 20-22, he said,

> **"If God will be with me and will watch over me on this journey I am taking and will give me food to eat and clothes to wear so that I return safely to my father's household, then the Lord will be my God and this stone that I have set up as a pillar will be God's house, and of all that you give me I will give you a tenth."**

In other words, at this point in his life, Jacob had not learned that a relationship with the living God of his father and grandfather was not something he could negotiate or control.

But that is something very difficult for a passive-aggressive person to accept.

The personal application for me comes in the memories I have of the times in my life when I also felt the presence of God strongly and heard His voice calling me to unconditionally receive His promises of love, acceptance, and provision. No matter how powerfully I felt His presence or how loudly I heard His voice, I had a tendency to add my own conditions. "If God would do this for me, then I would..." I would have never admitted that this was going on inside me at those times, but I now know it was.

My acceptance of God's full control of my life was never possible as long as I had those conditions lurking behind the commitments I was attempting to make. And conditions are an integral part of the passive-aggressive make-up.

It's a difficult thing to realize that the same dysfunction that brought pain and distance in my relationships with Kathy and the other people in my life can also bring pain and distance in my relationship with God. But once you see this truth, the clearer you can see the One waiting for you to reach the point where He can heal that dysfunction. As we will see, Jacob finally got there...and so did I.

THOUGHTS FROM KATHY

THE END RESULT OF GOD'S UNCONDITIONAL LOVE

After Boyd recognized his passive-aggressive tendencies and began to allow God to heal him, he was able to get hold of some spiritual truths that he had understood only with his head and not his heart. He now knows that even though God's love is unconditional, it includes a desire for us to be totally healed - no matter what we have to go through to get there.

8. What's Love Got To Do With It?

After his self-centeredness caused him to pass up a golden opportunity to allow God's Presence to bring healing to his life, Jacob continued his road trip to the land of his mother's family and ended up encountering the future love of his life at a shepherd's well. Genesis 29:1-14 tells of Jacob coming to a well where three flocks of sheep were waiting for the stone to be rolled from the mouth of the well so that they could drink. Jacob struck up a conversation with the shepherds and asked if they knew his mother's brother, Laban. While they were talking, a beautiful shepherdess arrived with her sheep, and the others told Jacob that she was the daughter of Laban.

When Jacob saw Rachel, the daughter of his uncle Laban, and Laban's sheep, he went over

**and rolled the stone away from the mouth
of the well and watered his uncle's sheep.
Then Jacob kissed Rachel and began to weep
aloud. He had told Rachel that he was a
relative of her father and a son of Rebekah.
So she ran and told her father.** (Genesis
29:10-12)

Even for men who operate with passive-aggressiveness as their
M.O., the physical and emotional attraction of a beautiful
woman can suddenly take them uncharacteristically out of
their own little world and cause them to desire what is best for
that woman. You see, passive-aggressive men typically default
to doing what is best for them, so it takes a seismic shift to
move them off of that game.

Jacob was simply having a fact-finding conversation with
some of the shepherds who had brought their flocks to the
well when he discovered that the gorgeous creature who was
approaching was none other than the daughter of his Uncle
Laban. Before he left home, Jacob had received specific instructions from his father regarding where he should find a
wife.

**So Isaac called for Jacob and blessed him.
Then he commanded him: "Do not marry**

a Canaanite woman. Go at once to Paddan Aram, to the house of your mother's father Bethuel. Take a wife for yourself there, from among the daughters of Laban, your mother's brother. (Genesis 28:1-2)

One of those daughters stood before him now, and his thoughts quickly centered on meeting her immediate need by rolling the large stone away from the well's mouth - a stone large enough that it normally took several shepherds to move it. This interruption of Jacob's usual self-centered ways provides an important glimpse into part of the cure for his and every other passive-aggressive man's dysfunction. When another person's needs can be seen as primary (meet them because of the other person) rather than secondary (meet them because of me), passive-aggressiveness takes a back seat.

I have to admit that I was struck by Kathy's beauty when I first met her, and the attraction I felt for her as our relationship grew did temporarily take me out of my little universe. *Temporarily* is the key word, because what she saw in me (or what I allowed her to see) was not a complete picture of who she would eventually end up with as a life partner.

The truth is that this may happen briefly in the lives of passive-aggressive men, especially when they're in the first throes of love, but putting another's needs first simply cannot last in the passive-aggressive universe. A deeper remedy is needed. Jacob would one day encounter that remedy, but first he would meet someone who could give him a large dose of his own passive-aggressive medicine.

THOUGHTS FROM KATHY

DYSFUNCTION IF I DO, AND DYSFUNCTION IF I DON'T

Passive-aggressive people tend to look for partners who are strong and make decisions easily. Then they won't have to make those decisions for themselves. You may not realize it at first, because it's not dumped on you all at once. They step out and let you make one decision at a time until you wake up one day with the weight of the world on your shoulders. I had to come to the point with Boyd where I realized that I was carrying far more than I should. Like most passive-aggressive men, he would use flattery. He would say, "That's your strength. You're so much better at finances (or making plans, etc.)" That's because he was happy for me to do the hard work of figuring out a budget or planning a trip. The problem came when he would come in at the last minute in order to get his way. I would try to lay down boundaries, but he wouldn't honor them. I even tried refusing to do those things so that he would have to. But I would usually end up taking the responsibility back, because I was exhausted with trying to get him to do his part. In other words, I couldn't win.

9. LOOKING IN THE MIRROR

After writing the previous chapter, it was more than two months before I could resume this study. The many parallels between the passive-aggressive tendencies of Jacob and what I've seen in my own life are sometimes just too much to handle to be able to move on easily to the next scene. However, I am convinced that what we will see in the remainder of Jacob's saga will bring both illumination and healing to those of us caught in a similar struggle.

We have now come to the point in the story that finds Jacob having to deal with another obviously passive-aggressive man, who happens to be the father of the young woman with whom Jacob had just been smitten. If we travel back a few chapters and decades, we see the very first mention of this man, only at that point it was in the role of Rebekah's brother when Abraham's servant came searching for a wife for Isaac.

The young woman ran and told her mother's household about these things. Now Rebekah had a brother named Laban, and he hurried out to the man at the spring. As soon as he had seen the nose ring, and the bracelets on his sister's arms, and had heard Rebekah tell what the man said to her, he went out to the man and found him standing by the camels near the spring. "Come, you who are blessed by the Lord," he said. "Why are you standing out here? I have prepared the house and a place for the camels." (Genesis 24:29-31)

I don't think it's inconsistent with the rest of the biblical narrative to see in this passage the seeds of some ulterior motives. It certainly appears that the sight of the obvious wealth represented by Abraham's servant caught Laban's attention very quickly. He may have simply been excited for his sister because he wanted the best for her. But could it be that this is a little preview of the ulterior motives seen in the classic tale of "bait and switch" in Genesis 29:15-29?

Perhaps Laban remembered seeing the nose ring and bracelets on his sister all those years ago and now realized that he had the chance to see some of that wealth attach itself to one of his daughters. The trouble came because he and Jacob just happened to have different daughters in mind.

Jacob thought he was making a deal to marry Rachel by agreeing to serve Laban for seven years. But when the time was up and the wedding night arrived, Laban put his older (and less beautiful) daughter, Leah, in Jacob's bed. Jacob, to whom the seven year wait **"seemed like only a few days"** because of his love for Rachel, inexplicably waited until the morning to realize that she was not the one lying beside him. Then he was forced to work seven more years for the daughter he had wanted in the first place.

We have to put aside the obvious questions regarding Jacob's lack of sensitivity in lovemaking that would allow him to mistake one sister for the other on his wedding night. The real question should focus on Laban, because in him we have an even more fine-tuned version of the passive-aggressive man. And that leads to a discussion of how one passive-aggressive man deals with another of the same tendencies.

I had not considered that the "bait and switch" tactic was a part of the passive-aggressive toolbox until I read this passage as part of the overall story of Jacob. But...I couldn't help noticing that Jacob offering stew to get what he wanted (the birthright) is really not that far from Laban offering Rachel to get what he wanted (a married Leah).

Let me break it down like this. A passive-aggressive man is more than aware of the needs or desires of the person or persons with whom he's relating. And many times he has the capacity to meet those needs or fulfill those desires. So, whether he says so or not, the passive-aggressive man gives the impression that he is going to do what needs to be done in a given situation. The trouble comes when his own needs or desires take center stage and become the true recipient of his actions.

Actually, as I've been pondering this portion of Jacob's life where God gives him a chance to look into a mirror named Laban and experience what it feels like to be on the receiving end of pure passive-aggression, I'm beginning to think that "bait and switch" might be the perfect terminology for the passive-aggressive M.O. And when a man who is used to baiting and switching becomes the victim of baiting and switching, it can be both a rude awakening and the impetus to begin to crawl out of his little universe to a place of healing.

I know that there have been times when I've dealt with passive-aggressive men within my own circle of relationships and seen how their promises, whether explicit or implicit, can morph into something entirely different than what I first understood. When you think you know someone well enough to trust that he will do what is best for everyone involved, including himself, but then turns it all around in order to feed his own fear or insecurity, the sense of betrayal catches you completely off-guard. I can now more clearly see and more readily admit that I've done that to Kathy and others in my life because it's been done to me as well.

So the mirror that can be put in front of a passive-aggressive man through the actions of another passive-aggressive man can be an eye-opening moment. It certainly has been that for me. It's sad that Scripture seems to indicate that Jacob didn't allow his experience with Laban to cause him to take a closer look at himself. That closer look was to come a little later, because Jacob's God was even then in the process of setting up an ambush.

THOUGHTS FROM KATHY

TRUST UNDONE

I would say that the worst part of living with a passive-aggressive man is how his actions destroy any trust that has been built between him and his partner.

There is absolutely nothing worse than being deceived by someone you should be able to trust. There have been many times when I've told Boyd that it would take a long time before I would be able to trust him again. One action (or inaction) coming from a passive-aggressive motivation can undo a thousand healthy actions.

Even small things contribute to this lack of trust. I remember going into situations thinking that Boyd and I were on the same page, but I would somehow always be left holding the ball because he wouldn't express his opinion. We would agree ahead of time regarding what we were going to say, but I was the only one who ended up talking...even when I asked him, "What do you think about that?" It's a helpless feeling, and it destroys trust.

10. Unvalidated Emotions

The next scene in our story centers around the contrast of Rachel's inability and Leah's ability to bear children with Jacob. Leah's womb was quickly productive with four sons in a row while Rachel watched and waited for her chance to be a mother. Chapter 30 of Genesis begins with a revealing conversation:

> **Now when Rachel saw that she bore Jacob no children, Rachel envied her sister, and said to Jacob, "Give me children, or else I die!" — And Jacob's anger was aroused against Rachel, and he said, "Am I in the place of God, who has withheld from you the fruit of the womb?" (Genesis 30:1-2)**

It is a rare occurrence in the life of a passive-aggressive man to be able to say his "anger was aroused", because he's typically careful to keep his anger under lock and key. But the exchange captured in this passage reveals the one hot button that can bring about this rare outward show of anger.

When someone in relationship with a passive-aggressive man expresses legitimate anger, that expression of anger triggers something within the passive-aggressive psyche that calls forth a response laced with anger that is not passive. This response is designed to do one thing - delegitimize the other person's anger.

I will admit to doing this many times when Kathy has expressed anger over a situation in our lives. I think it was a protective mechanism that kicked in so that I wouldn't have to face the fact that I didn't have the ability to express anger in a healthy way like she did. I can remember often verbally stopping her from venting completely by expressing anger of my own - not because what she was saying was wrong, but because it made me uncomfortable to be in the presence of anger expressed in a constructive way. By doing so, I effectively delegitimized her anger - and kept my own little dysfunctional universe intact.

This is just the opposite of the usual scenario, where Kathy would do or say something that would make me mad, but I would bury that anger until a later time when it would come lurching out of the grave in some subconscious passive-aggressive form of punishment. The difference is the emotion behind the guilty action. If Kathy simply did or said something that bothered me without her anger attached to it, my anger response typically went underground. But if her deeds or words were accompanied by a show of anger, my outward show of anger came into play and threw water on the fire before it could spread into my world and shed the light of truth on the situation.

A passive-aggressive man has to learn to verbally legitimize the anger of his partner or others in his life. Saying "I can understand why you feel that way" is a helpful addition to the vocabulary of a man who doesn't major in either understanding or feelings. Allowing anger to be expressed in his presence without having to counter with a larger dose of his own is a huge step toward healing.

If Jacob had expressed concern for Rachel's feelings and an understanding of what she was going through, their relationship would have experienced healing and Rachel might have been spared a lot of emotional trauma as she watched her sister and the handmaidens of both women bear Jacob children. An understanding husband might have given her the foundation to rest in God and wait for His plan to unfold.

On the other hand, in those situations where the anger tends to get buried after someone does or says something that the passive-aggressive man perceives as wrong or hurtful, the very best thing to do is to admit to that anger in a healthy way as soon as possible after the offense takes place. The other person has no way of knowing what you are feeling unless you explain it to them. Saying "I need to tell you why what you did makes me angry" is another tool that can be used to keep anger aboveground where it needs to stay.

Thoughts From Kathy

Stirred Up

I can identify with how angry Rachel was in this passage, because passive-aggressiveness stirs up anger. There have been many times I have asked Boyd to meet a particular need, thinking it would be natural for him to do so as my partner. When I found out that he never met that need, it would stir up a certain amount of anger within me. This would happen time after time, and the anger that came out of each incident would pile up until it had to be expressed. Then the real harm would take place when Boyd would turn the whole thing around to look like it was my problem because I expressed anger. Or he wouldn't partner with me in a situation and carry his part. The reason that stirred up so much anger is the fact that he wouldn't take responsibility for himself or validate my feelings when I would have real emotions because of his actions.

11. Avoiding Responsibilty

As I read the next part of chapter 30, I reviewed with interest poor Jacob's trials as he was "forced" to have sex with two additional women because of the rivalry between his wives. At first glance, I saw no signs of his passive-aggression in this part of the story. However, something began to dawn on me. Look at what happened after the exchange between Jacob and Rachel we just examined.

Genesis 30:3-24 recounts how Rachel told Jacob to have sex with her maid, Bilhah, and the two sons that resulted. Then Leah decided to play the same game by giving Jacob her maid, Zilpah, with whom he had two more sons. Following this, Leah traded some mandrakes in exchange for Rachel's permission for her to again sleep with Jacob. Leah, who had stopped bearing children before this, was once again blessed with a son. She followed this with another son and a daughter. Then Rachel finally became pregnant and gave birth to Joseph.

One of the passive-aggressive man's tendencies is to allow the desires and decisions of others to control the circumstances of his life. That may sound odd for someone who is so self-centered. But the key to understanding this lies in the fact that a passive aggressive man almost always wants the responsibility for a decision to lie on someone else's shoulders. By avoiding the responsibility, he avoids the blame when something goes wrong. I said he "almost" always does this, because there are times when he knows a decision will bring a good result and is very willing to take the accolades for that result. Plus, he often finds a way to take back the responsibility for a decision he was unwilling to make when it is discovered to have been the correct one, thereby stripping the one who actually made the decision of his or her right to be praised. There have been more times than I want to admit when I found myself taking credit for a good decision only to be reminded by my wife that she had planted the idea in the first place. I had simply chosen to leave that bit of information out of my analysis of the situation.

In other words (and this is just as difficult for me to write as it is for those of you who are like me to read), passive-aggressive men have a responsibility deficit. That leads to a life lived without direction or purpose. As was the case with Jacob, unless God steps in to change things, the passive-aggressive man will allow his own reluctance to take responsibility to keep him from living his life to the full.

The rest of chapter 30 details an interesting situation that took place between Jacob and Laban. Once again, the passive-aggressive tendencies of both men take center stage. I want to explore the initial exchange between the two here with the remainder of the story to follow in the next segment.

After Rachel gave birth to Joseph, Jacob said to Laban, "Send me on my way so I can go back to my own homeland. Give me my wives and children, for who I have served you, and I will be on my way. You know how much work I've done for you." But Laban said to him, "If I have found favor in your eyes, please stay. I have learned by divination that the Lord has blessed me because of you." He added, "Name your wages, and I will pay them." Jacob said to him, "You know how I have worked for you and how your livestock has fared under my care. The little you had before I came has increased greatly, and the Lord has blessed you wherever I have been.

But now, when may I do something for my own household?" (Genesis 30:25-29)

When I first read this passage and the verses following it, I got lost in the details and failed to see the underlying motives of both men. First of all, Jacob had every right to tell Laban that he was taking his family and going back to his own country. He had served his time for both Rachel and Leah, and there was nothing holding him there. Of course, it would have been right for him to communicate his intentions to Laban clearly, since it was Laban's daughters and grandchildren who would be leaving with him. However, Jacob took it one step farther by asking Laban to send him away. Once again, Jacob as a passive-aggressive man wanted the decision to be made by someone else. Far be it from him to take responsibility for his own actions and destiny! If that sounds like someone you know, then that someone probably has passive-aggressive tendencies.

The problem for Jacob arose because he was dealing with the passive-aggressiveness of Laban, who begged him to stay and, in a rare moment of candor, revealed that his motives for wanting Jacob to stay went beyond a desire to keep his family close. Laban admitted that Jacob's presence had brought blessing to him, and he quite frankly did not want to lose that blessing. So he told Jacob to name his price.

Jacob used this revelation to his advantage by agreeing with Laban's assessment of their arrangement and even clarifying it by reminding Laban of how little he had before Jacob came and how much he had after the years he had worked for him. But he didn't answer Laban's request to name his wages. Instead, he asked when he would be able to provide for his own house. This is also a typical scenario in a passive-aggressive man's life.

For some reason, it is difficult for this type of man to step up and say exactly what is on his mind or to be definitive regarding his desires. He almost always wraps those desires up in a secondary or indirect communication. Instead of saying that he had decided to take his wives and children and move back home, Jacob involved Laban in a discussion about his worth to Laban's business and then wondered out loud how long it would be before he could independently provide for his own family. This was once again an attempt to force Laban to make Jacob's life decisions for him.

Now, we can put it all together. The seemingly innocuous tendency to allow others to make his decisions for him becomes relationally deadly for those dealing with the passive-aggressive man when coupled with the trap he sets by his indirect communication. In other words, this type of man actually knows what he wants before he ever begins the communication cycle, but his dysfunction causes him to seek the result he wants through manipulating others to come around to his viewpoint - a viewpoint that he's not willing to fully express or defend.

This manifests itself in a variety of ways, both large and small. Let's begin with the small. The simple act of deciding where to go out and eat is a microcosm of this dysfunction. When a passive-aggressive man is asked where he wants to eat, his first line is: "I don't care." This is actually a lie, because whether or not he consciously acknowledges it at the time, he does care. He has an opinion, and he has a way of working that opinion into the conversation later. There have been times when I've actually agreed to a dining destination suggested by Kathy but found myself pointing out other possibilities on the way to the chosen spot. Kathy has learned to simply not be the first one to suggest a restaurant unless she truly has a strong preference, and I have learned to come to a mutual decision and not a manipulated one.

Apply this same principle to larger decisions, like where to live or where to go to church or how to raise children or how to deal with in-laws, and the game of manipulation becomes deadly. I truly wish I didn't have the memories of holding back when decisions (big and small) were made, the only reason being that I didn't want to take   stances that would make me look bad in the eyes of my family or other people in my circle. Too many times my lack of speaking out against dangerous decisions my children, Tanna and Asher, were making contributed to unwanted outcomes, some extremely negative and life-altering. The passive side of the passive-aggressive dysfunction can often be more destructive than the eventual aggressiveness. The sad truth is that deep down I almost always knew the right thing to do or say but chose not to do so.

The rest of the narrative recounting the manipulation and counter-manipulation between Jacob and his father-in-law will be our next stop, and it will give us a closer look at the odd chemistry that takes place when passive-aggressive men work together. But the initial exchange that we just detailed is the key to understanding the motives of these two passive-aggressive poster boys.

THOUGHTS FROM KATHY

STOP THE GAME

A counselor once shared a word picture with me that I've never forgotten. He said that a marriage that is going through some problems can be seen as a basketball game where two teams are playing, and the scoreboard suddenly stops working. One coach wants to continue playing the game, but the other coach takes his or her players off the court and says they won't get back in the game until the scoreboard is fixed.

A passive-aggressive person is simply not using the same scoreboard as his or her partner. So that partner has to stop the game and announce, "The scoreboard isn't working. I'm taking my team (what I bring to the relationship) off the court until we can get the scoreboard fixed." That forces the passive-aggressive person to decide whether or not to be part of a healthy and functional partnership. Sometimes I've actually said those words to Boyd, and other times I've just used this picture to help position myself so that his passive-aggressiveness had to stop its dysfunctional cycle.

12. WHITTLING A WORLD OF HIS OWN

In Genesis 30:30-43 we get to observe passive-aggressive manhood at a high level of intensity. The inability of Jacob and Laban to simply communicate with each other regarding their situation led to a long, drawn-out game of manipulation.

When Laban asked Jacob what he wanted, Jacob offered up quite a unique bargain. He asked Laban to simply allow him to take the speckled and spotted sheep, the brown lambs, and the spotted and speckled goats out of Laban's flocks. In other words, instead of asking Laban for an amount of wages for the work he's been doing, he would take just these specific animals from the flocks. Anything else found in his possession would be treated as stolen.

Laban was quick to accept this deal. He gathered up all the animals which fit the description Jacob had given him and had his sons take them three days' journey away from Jacob. He wasn't taking any chances.

But this didn't deter Jacob. He took some rods of the poplar, almond, and chestnut trees and peeled some white strips in them. Then he set those "spotted and speckled" rods in front of the flocks where they came to drink and to conceive their young. What the flocks conceived in front of those rods turned out to be spotted and speckled as well, making them Jacob's possessions. He even went so far as to allow only the strong animals to conceive in front of those rods, giving him the very best of the flocks and Laban the leftovers.

This passage can be confusing if you concentrate on the details rather than the concepts or focus on the trees rather than the forest. After hovering over the story for some time, I finally began to see the underlying passive-aggressive tendencies. And these tendencies come out quite regularly when one passive-aggressive man has to deal with another passive-aggressive man.

The first tendency I saw was territorial. Throughout this passage, Jacob and Laban actually fought to claim their own territory within their relationship. Jacob used creativity and deception, and Laban employed distance, but both attempted to enlarge their territory at the expense of the other.

This is typical when passive-aggressive men work together at a job or for a cause. What they don't know is how much easier it would be for both of them if they used their abilities to complement each other in order to do a better job or further their cause. The sad truth is that passive-aggressive men would rather see something they are involved in, whether it be a job, a cause, or a personal relationship, fail than to give up their territorial ways to work together. This is also why passive-aggressive men in leadership have a difficult time unless those under their leadership are weaker than they are. When faced with an obviously stronger personality (or even an equally strong one), they find themselves threatened, and rather than be effective leaders who summon all the parts of an organization together, they squelch what could be the organization's greatest assets.

Jacob and Laban could have come to an agreement that would have been beneficial for both, but neither was willing to work toward such an agreement. And although it looked like Jacob came out on top in this case, the damage done to his relationship with his father-in-law (and probably his wives as well) far outweighed any victory he may have gained.

I have worked on projects with other passive-aggressive men where I knew that my contribution would be essential to success. However, when my contribution was offered (and most likely undergirded with my own territorial slant), the other passive-aggressive men felt their own territory threatened. In the passive-aggressive world, this does not lead to an upfront rejection, but rather an initial acceptance of the contribution which is followed by no further action to help coordinate it with the overall project. Since saying an immediate "no" goes against the easy-going persona he has built, a passive-aggressive man in leadership will say "yes", whether verbal or implied, to someone else's ideas. However, that someone else will most likely never be called on to put those ideas into action.

By the way, this is the key to understanding how a passive-aggressive man can seem to take seriously his partner's contribution to a decision but then leave that contribution behind when the decision is actually made. In both cases, it all comes down to protecting his own territory, which keeps him from being able to truly partner with someone else.

Now, Laban couldn't let Jacob be the only player in this game. While Jacob used an elaborate scheme to further his territory, Laban simply put miles (or actually three days' journey) between them. He gave his sons the livestock that would be favorable to Jacob and sent them as far away as he could. This action not only shows the territorial tendency of this very passive-aggressive man, but it also falls into the withholding category I explored early on in this study. Laban withheld the very things that would bring Jacob success. Of course, by this time, there was not even a pretense of working together. They were obviously at odds, so the withholding was a natural part of the game. The more harmful withholding takes place in relationships or in the workplace where the two parties are supposed to be working toward the same goal. In those cases, the weapon of withholding is used not to harm a foe but to stab a friend in the back.

The portion of this story where Jacob took rods from the trees around him and peeled white spots in them so that the livestock would breed spotted and speckled offspring by looking at those rods was the greatest challenge of all for me. I tried for a long time to see a way this applied to passive-aggressiveness. It finally came to me. Passive-aggressive men cut into or change or manipulate the environment around them in order to breed whatever is best for their personal little universe. I'm not saying that this was the main intent of the Inspirer of this passage of Scripture. However, when it's used as a symbol of the M.O. of a passive-aggressive man, it is absolutely stunning!

I know that I still do a little passive-aggressive whittling here and there, so I'm hoping this picture of Jacob literally carving out his own world will haunt me until I drop my pocket-knife in the dirt and walk away forever. Again, I'm not being oblivious to the fact that Jacob's trick won the day, but victory has to be judged by its cost. I no longer want to win at the expense of far more important things.

THOUGHTS FROM KATHY

GET OFF THE RUG

There are so many horrible emotions attached to dealing with a passive-aggressive man. The only way I've been able to describe how it feels is to use word pictures. The one that has helped me the most, especially in telling Boyd how his passive-aggressiveness affected me, is the picture of a rug being pulled out from under me. I could be going along pretty well, thinking that my relationship with Boyd was good, and then something would happen to jar me back to the reality that I was living with someone who, in one situation, could pull the rug of my emotional balance out from under me. In the worst situations, that pulled rug could also feel like a knife in the back.

13. THE UNFAVORABLE FACE

We find a phrase used in the beginning of Genesis chapter 31 that once again shines the light on the passive-aggressive dynamic. The phrase was actually used by Jacob as he attempted to give a description of his deteriorating relationship with Laban. He had heard some of Laban's sons talking about how Jacob had taken away their father's wealth. The words of verse 2 jumped off the page at me:

> **"And Jacob saw the countenance of Laban, and indeed it was not favorable toward him as before."**

Combined with a word from God, this gave Jacob the extra little push he needed to decide to return home. He even explained to his wives in verse 5 what he had seen in their father, and he used the same word:

"I see your father's countenance, that it is not favorable toward me as before; but the God of my father has been with me."

This translation from the New King James Version may sound a bit old-fashioned, and it is changed in many other versions to something that refers to Laban's change of "attitude". I'm sure there was a change in attitude, but I think staying with the original Hebrew, which said that Jacob saw that Laban's "panim" or "countenance" or "face" was not as before, provides a helpful visual.

Jacob obviously saw something in the way Laban looked at him that gave away what was inside his heart and mind. Maybe it was a grimace or an eye twitch or a twisting of the neck. Or maybe it was something far more subtle and far deeper...and yet something that could be seen or sensed. Whatever it was, it shook Jacob to his core and made it much easier to hear the voice of God telling him to get out of town.

I don't want to make too much of this, but I know that look from the inside just as Kathy has experienced it from the outside. Because the anger of passive-aggressive men often gets stuffed into an emotional closet for a period of time, whenever that closet gets full, its contents have to start spilling out. I've felt that moment happen many times when something Kathy or someone else does is simply the last straw, leaving no more room to push an uninvited emotion away. That emotion seems to hang right there in front of your face, forcing you to deal with it. When you do, the dam breaks, and the flood of blaming and punishing thoughts you've kept at bay for so long now comes out. And the very first change signaling this process happens right there on your face. No matter how hard you try to control it, a thoughtful observer can see it clearly.

I was having lunch with a friend a few years ago, and in our conversation about my journey out of passive-aggression, he asked me if I knew when I was operating in it or if it was an overall lifestyle. I believe that before I saw and admitted that I was a carrier of this emotional disease, I was mostly unaware of its working in my life because it had become so much of the fabric of my thoughts and actions. However, now that I've been in the process of coming to grips with the destructive nature of passive-aggression for the past twenty years, I can definitely sense it as it begins to try to work in me again. I can literally see from the inside a change come over my face. And I'm quite sure Kathy can recognize it from a mile away. In other words, it's very difficult for me to get by with anything that even starts to look or sound or smell like passive-aggression.

In the remainder of the passage, Jacob told Rachel and Leah how their father had deceived him. It makes me wonder if those two sisters might have looked at each other with knowing glances. Jacob was not exactly innocent in the deception department, and I wouldn't doubt that both of these ladies may have been on the receiving end of some of that deception. You see, Jacob was seeing the changing "countenance" of his father-in-law while neglecting to see his own. I started to use the famous picture Jesus used of the speck and the log, but in this case I'm afraid there were two logs.

Jacob also sees that God had not allowed Laban's trickery to harm him. And he was also somehow able to hear God tell him that it was time to leave. I do believe God was working in this situation to push Jacob out of a comfortable rut and into a little different trajectory - a trajectory that would lead straight into a confrontation with Someone who was a far more formidable opponent than his father-in-law.

Thoughts From Kathy

Stopping It In Its Tracks

I used to be surprised by the passive-aggressive stuff operating in Boyd, because many times I didn't see it coming. Lately I've been able to catch the first hint of it and stop it before it pulls me into its trap. It may be the look on his face or the tone of his voice, but somehow I know where it's heading. That has made a difference for me and has kept us from going too far down the wrong road.

14. THE WOMAN DRIVEN TO IDOLS

As I read the next scenes in Jacob's story, I found the spotlight shifting from our passive-aggressive protagonist to one of his wives. Tucked away in the middle of the next few scenes is a very interesting picture of how women who are married to passive-aggressive men typically deal with their situation. Let me give you an overview of these scenes and then focus in on one very interesting detail that speaks to our subject.

After realizing that God had allowed him to have the upper hand in his dealings with Laban, Jacob told his wives about a dream in which God commanded him to return to his own land. Rachel and Leah agreed to go with him, because they saw that their father had turned his back on them and that his riches were now in the hands of Jacob. As the family left without telling Laban, Rachel took the idols that belonged to her father's house.

When Laban discovered that his daughters and grandchildren had left with Jacob, he mounted a posse and took off after them. After a seven day journey, he caught up with them, but by this time he had been warned by God in a dream to speak neither good nor bad to Jacob. He did ask his son-in-law why he left secretly and why he stole his idols. Jacob obviously did not know about Rachel's "klepto-moment", because he told Laban to kill anyone who was found with the idols.

So Laban began his search, and this is how the next scene is recorded in Genesis 31:33-35:

> **So Laban went into Jacob's tent and into Leah's tent and into the tent of the two female servants, but he found nothing. After he came out of Leah's tent, he entered Rachel's tent. Now Rachel had taken the household gods and put them inside her camel's saddle and was sitting on them. Laban searched through everything in the tent but found nothing. Rachel said to her father, "Don't be angry, my lord, that I cannot stand up in your presence; I'm having my period." So he searched but could not find the household gods.**

Jacob took this awkward occasion to berate Laban regarding all the things he had put him through and made clear to him that the God of his fathers had kept him safe from Laban's schemes. Laban responded by initiating a covenant with Jacob and commemorating it with a heap of stones that would be a barrier between them. Verses 51 through 53 tell it like this:

> **Laban also said to Jacob, "Here is this heap, and here is this pillar I have set up between you and me. This heap is a witness, and this pillar is a witness, that I will not go past this heap to your side to harm you and that you will not go past this heap and pillar to my side to harm me. May the God of Abraham and the God of Nahor, the God of their father, judge between us."**

Although this last part of the story is not my main point right now, I have to say that these two passive-aggressive men hit the nail right on the head when they put up a boundary between each other. One of the most important things that anyone dealing with passive-aggressive men, especially their partners, can learn is how to erect boundaries that keep this dysfunction from spilling over into territory that does not belong to them. Kathy has learned this lesson very well, and

I still occasionally bump up against piles of stones that are clearly marked to keep my passive-aggressive tendencies from coming back over to her side.

Speaking of Kathy, I now need to separate the way she has dealt with me from the way most partners of passive-aggressive men deal with their dysfunctional other half. To do that, I want to return to the scene in Rachel's tent where she was sitting on the stolen, and now hidden, idols from her father's house. Rachel showed her own adeptness at deception as she fooled her own father - and without her husband's knowledge. She had found a way to meet some of her own needs in the midst of the battle between the two most important men in her life.

When I thought about the picture of this woman beaten down by years of living with two passive-aggressive men having to pile deception on top of stealing in order to keep her own little tent from being destroyed, I was amazed at how accurately this depicts most women who deal with passive-aggressive men. After Kathy and I began to work through our relationship, we started seeing more and more couples trapped in the same dynamic. And most of the partners in those relationships have not chosen to openly deal with the truth like Kathy has.

Like Rachel, many of these partners find themselves creating their own little tent out of lies and deception, because they have found that the tents put up by their passive-aggressive men typically don't have room for more than one person. They will begin to look to other things or people to provide what their partner's dysfunction won't allow him to provide. They find it easier to look past that dysfunction rather than confronting it and dealing with it.

But in order to do that, they must sew together a tent strong enough to keep the real problem outside. That tent may be made of friends, hobbies, jobs, etc. Its fabric may be finding worth in serving others to the point of exhaustion - but at least that leaves no time to see the real situation. Some of those tents may be put up within the walls of the church - a place that is sadly not a stranger to people who want to exchange the truth of their own lives for doing God's work.

The saddest part of this picture is that they end up using lies and deception to move away from the lies and deception used by their dysfunctional partner. As they sit inside their tent straddling the things they now think will make their life work (and is that not what idols are advertised to do?), they are completely unaware that their tent has been staked out in the sand.

What they need to do is to get up from the things that have promised to give them life, walk out of their tent and over to the tent of their partner, and proceed to pull out every stake that holds his little tent together. That is what my wife did, and I will always love her for having the courage to do it.

Thoughts From Kathy

The Codependent Trap

One of the questions the partner of a passive-aggressive man has to ask is: What kind of dysfunction do I have that has allowed his dysfunction to become such an issue in our lives? Boyd came into our marriage as a passive-aggressive man. I didn't make him one. But I had to come to the realization that there was something in my life and history that allowed his passive-aggressiveness to operate. When you enter into a relationship with someone who has a dysfunction that feeds on the dysfunction in your life, you have to make a decision. You can either stand up and refuse to operate in the dysfunction, or you can adapt to it and lose part of yourself in the process. The reason a person in a relationship with a passive-aggressive man chooses to adapt is the fact that he seems like such a nice guy. So when his passive-aggressiveness comes out of hiding, it drags his partner into a place of enabling his dysfunction.

The key is to not allow yourself to become a victim, because victimization excuses the other person's problem.

Allowing yourself to become a victim is the same as saying that God is not big enough to change your situation or heal what is wrong in your relationship. You have to simply become responsible for yourself, and then everything else takes care of itself. You must tell your dysfunctional partner that you're not playing the game. You're not crossing the line to become responsible for him. If you participate in someone else's dysfunction, you're taking the place of God. You're covering his sins, and you're not allowing him to become whole.

15. DESPERATION AND THE SPLIT

As we slide into Genesis chapter 32 and approach the climactic moment in Jacob's life - the one which pictures the cure for his (and every other passive-aggressive man's) dysfunction - we see a terribly desperate man trying on his own to deal with the devastation that dysfunction had caused to his relationship with his twin brother many years before.

The chapter begins by saying that Jacob met some angels while he was on his way and proclaimed **"This is God's camp."** Then he sent messengers ahead to tell Esau about his wealth (a hint of a bribe) for the purpose **"that I mind favor in your eyes."** (verse 5) The messengers returned and told Jacob that Esau was headed his way with four hundred men. Needless to say, this stirred up a considerable amount of emotion in Jacob - one emotion specifically...fear.

What Jacob did next is quite interesting. He divided the people and animals that were with him into two companies. He said in verse 8,

"If Esau comes and attacks one group, then the other group that is left may escape."

Just for good measure, he added a prayer to his plan (notice the order - plan followed by prayer). He even reminded God of His earlier promises. Jacob's next faith-filled action was to send a succession of presents, large numbers of animals, ahead to his brother.

Two things stand out in this peek into Jacob's fear-filled brain. First of all, he was especially desirous of getting on Esau's good side as quickly as possible. He sent messengers ahead in verse 5 with instructions to begin the groveling process in order to **"find favor"** in Esau's sight. Then came the sending ahead of a present. Verse 20 gives the clearest view of his inner workings at the time:

"I will pacify him with these gifts I am sending on ahead; later, when I see him; perhaps he will receive me."

Jacob was obviously hoping for a reaction from Esau that would not be a justified response to what he had done to his twin brother those years ago. Instead of revenge, he wanted Esau to show him favor and acceptance.

I'm not sure Jacob would have wagered very much on that being the case, because when he heard from his messengers upon their return that Esau was coming his way with four hundred men, he decided to divide his family into two parts and accept the loss of whichever half Esau attacked - if Esau indeed chose attack rather than acceptance. And this pictures pretty graphically another tactic of passive-aggressive men.

When passive-aggression is in full bloom, it has an extraordinary way of finding every conceivable path to manipulation and control. Plus, when the passive-aggressive host (and I mean that in every possible shade of meaning) sees a confrontation coming with one of his victims, he often splits himself into two different companies - just like Jacob. He may try responding with penitence and apology but all the while be quite assured that he was in the right and ready to defend his actions. And if the high road doesn't get him to his destination, he is more than happy to take the low one.

What is more than just a little bit scary about what I just wrote is that I didn't know its full extent until I finished writing it. I knew the two camps Jacob sent out was a picture of a passive-aggressive mindset, but I didn't quite know what it was until I thought back through a good number of scenes in my relationship with Kathy where I did exactly what I was picturing as the two companies sent out to meet the offended party. I've done that more times than I want to admit as I've come back to my offended wife with my sackcloth of repentance covering up a full suit of the armor of defending what I did. And just like Jacob, if one of those companies gets attacked, I still had the other one to fall back on.

Ouch, that hurt! Why am I doing this? Oh, yes. I know there are many men (and their victims) who can find freedom and healing through my transparency. But that still doesn't make it stop hurting.

Anyway, I said there were two things that stand out in this passage. Number two is that although Jacob immediately recognized through the presence of angels that the place he was stopping was "God's camp" (verse 1), his first communication with God was a reminder of God's promise to deal well with him (verse 9) and a plea for protection from the wrath of his brother (verse 11). In other words, although it was God's camp, Jacob was still laying out the terms.

A vital truth for any person, and especially for someone with passive-aggressive tendencies, is that God is not someone who can be manipulated or controlled. Jacob was right in calling the place where his feet hit the ground at that point in his life

"God's camp".   And he was just about to find out exactly what that meant.

THOUGHTS FROM KATHY

LOVE MEANS NEVER HAVING TO SAY...

When a passive-aggressive man comes to you with an apology, it's important that you look beyond his words. He's a lot like an alcoholic who seems on the outside to have a desire to change but still has something raging inside of him that has far more control over him than his words.

16. The Place of Emptying

So now we come to the climax in the story of Jacob's life and finally to the basic solution to the dysfunction his story has pictured for us. What follows is one of the most fascinating passages in all of Scripture, so I'm quoting the whole thing before we examine it.

> That night Jacob got up and took his two wives, his two female servants, and his eleven sons, and crossed the ford of the Jabbok. After he had sent them across the stream, he sent over all his possessions. So Jacob was left alone, and a man wrestled with him till daybreak. When the man saw that he could not overpower him, he touched the socket of Jacob's hip so that his hip was wrenched as he wrestled with the man. Then the man

said, "Let me go, for it is daybreak." But Jacob replied, "I will not let you go unless you bless me." The man asked him, "What is your name?" "Jacob," he answered. Then the man said, "Your name will no longer be Jacob, but Israel, because you have struggled with God and with humans, and have overcome." Jacob said, "Please tell me your name." But he replied, "Why do you ask my name?" Then he blessed him there. So Jacob called the place Peniel, saying, "It is because I saw God face to face, and yet my life was spared." The sun rose above him as he passed Peniel, and he was limping because of his hip. Therefore to this day the Israelites do not eat the tendon attached to the socket of the hip, because the socket of Jacob's hip was touched near the tendon. (Genesis 32:22-31)

Before we shift our attention to the strangest wrestling match ever, we need to look down at the water gurgling over the rocks as we imagine Jacob sending his family across the ford, which would have been one of the most shallow places of the river, and then staying on the opposite side in order to have a place of solitude. The name of the brook or river was Jabbok, which means "an emptying out" or "a wrestling". Both of those meanings are appropriate for that spiritual moment in Jacob's journey. The "wrestling" connection is obvious from what follows. But I want to focus for a bit on the "emptying out", because it points us to one of the key steps in bringing a passive-aggressive man to the point of finding healing.

I've told you about how the protection of my own little universe was a large part of my motivation for many years. I believe this is true of all passive-aggressive men. We live inside of what we think is reality but is actually an illusion of our own making. Kathy has pointed out several times the absolute absurdity of some of my actions or decisions over the years, and I now realize they were coming from an environment founded on my own manipulation of reality.

I believe a passive-aggressive man has an initial decision to make before he can deal with his dysfunction. That decision goes far deeper than mental assent to a truth. It is the gut-wrenching, internal choice to "empty" out the unreal world in which he has operated for so long so that the real world can take its place. For me, it was coming to a point where I had to do more than admit that there was a problem. I had to be willing to turn my world upside down in order to see what was really out there. Like Jacob, I found myself on the banks of a river that was an obvious turning point in my life. Kathy had guided me (and sometimes pushed me) to that river, but she didn't have the power to make me cross. I hope every reader who is the partner of a passive-aggressive man just underlined that last sentence. Jacob sent his wives and family on across the river, because he had to face all by himself the decision to walk out of his universe and into another. That's when the true Ultimate Wrestler showed His beautiful game Face.

Thoughts From Kathy

How Much Longer?

Holding your ground long enough for your partner to finally come to the place where he's willing to face his stuff is one of the most difficult things you'll ever do.

17. THE WOUND OF HEALING

O nce the decision is made to dump the unreality of our manipulated universe into the waters of the Jabbok, passive-aggressive men are faced with a scary thought. If our identities have been built on a faulty foundation, then who are we? Where do we go to find the truth about ourselves? Our partners and others who love us can help us see who we're not, but they don't have the power to give us identity. As was the case with Jacob, there is only One Who can give us a new name.

The text says that when Jacob was left alone, "a man wrestled with him till daybreak." Some translations capitalize the "M" in Man, reflecting both the context and the historical understanding of the passage. This was no ordinary man. Nor was it merely an angelic appearance. His wrestling Partner suggested that Jacob had "struggled with God", and Jacob himself said that he had "seen God face to face". So God

Himself stepped into the midst of Jacob's "emptying out" to offer a new identity, one built on the greatest reality - the name reserved for him within the heart of God.

There are so many spiritual truths in this passage that I'm falling all over myself trying to get to them. Please be patient.

One of those truths was hidden within the action of the story until I saw it in light of the very first picture of passive-aggressiveness seen in the life of Jacob. Do you remember how Jacob grabbed Esau's heel coming out of the womb? This is a striking analogy to the manipulations of passive-aggressive men. I saw it in my own life, as I've come from behind and seized control of situations by utilizing the energy of the person I want to control.

Now, take that picture and contrast it to Jacob holding onto to his divine Opponent in this moonlit wrestling match. Could it be that Jacob's only lasting hold was the man's heel as He was attempting to leave at the breaking of day? Could it be that those famous words **"I will not let You go unless You bless me"** were uttered from the ground as Jacob held on for dear life to the heel of God? And could it be that this is the goal in the evolution of those of us who are heel-grabbers - to stop controlling life by utilizing the energy of the people around us and harness instead the energy of the One Person who is beyond our control and yet allows us to establish that hold in order to be the One from Whom we receive every direction?

In other words, heel-grabbing is not necessarily a bad practice when we are grabbing the correct Heel.

Three more things happened after Jacob demanded his blessing. First of all, he was given a new name. He was changed from "Heel-Grabber" to "He Who Struggles or Wrestles with God". The very identity of the passive-aggressive man has to be switched from a concentration on grabbing the heels of the people around him in order to get his needs met to grabbing the Heel of God in order to receive the blessing of God. This new identity is so important that I will cover it in detail in chapters 19 through 22. For now it is simply the first of three observations about this incredible scene.

The second thing was the naming of the place where Jacob saw God "face-to-face". "Peniel" means "the face of God", so Jacob named the spot where he was changed Peniel. It is interesting to me that the persistence of Jacob in grabbing this appearance of God as He was attempting to go did not leave him with an emphasis on the lower part of His Body (the legs, the feet, the heel) but rather on His Face. That is the wonderful grace of God, because all of His dealings with us (even the painful ones) are meant to lead us to His wonderful Face.

Thirdly, during the struggle, Jacob's loving Adversary touched the socket of his hip and put it out of joint so that Jacob limped the rest of his life in memory of that moment. I believe that the passive-aggressive man who allows his Father to wrestle him into wholeness will come out of the struggle with a limp of some sort. I know now that the truth about how my dysfunction has harmed my family and friends will always be there to remind me that I cannot allow that dysfunction to control me again. And if the weakness in the legs of my spirit consistently cause me to fall on the ground, I will forever be grateful for each chance to again see the Heel of God - the one and only Heel I'm free to grab, because that Heel leads me to His Face.

THOUGHTS FROM KATHY

CHANGE IS POSSIBLE!

There's been a big change in Boyd's life, and it's truly made a difference in our life together. It's obvious to me that most of the time he recognizes the symptoms of his passive-aggressiveness before it can get a foothold in our relationship. If we do have an issue, we're able to talk it through without getting into that old vicious cycle, making it easier for Boyd to stop any destructive behavior.

18. Consequences and Blessings

Although the story of Jacob continues for the remainder of Genesis, I will end my analysis here at Peniel. Jacob soon discovered that his brother was not as angry with him as he had feared. More blessings and prosperity awaited him as he returned home. Sadly, he saw his dysfunction passed down to his sons, some of them taking it to new and creative levels with the slaughter of the newly-circumcised Shechemites and through the cover-up of the disappearance of his favorite son, Joseph.

But when all was said and done, Jacob's greatest moment was found in taking the blessing of naming he had experienced at Peniel and passing it on to his sons. The most poignant New Testament remembrance of Jacob's life is in Hebrews 11:21:

"By faith Jacob, when he was dying, blessed each of the sons of Joseph, and worshiped, leaning on the top of his staff."

Even in giving the blessing, Jacob's hip was there as a reminder of the wrestling match which changed his life forever.

I don't want to give the impression that a one-time spiritual experience will transform a passive-aggressive man overnight. Jacob still had his issues, and so do I. But the God who revealed Himself as Jacob's Answer has done the same for me. Another important distinction is the fact that Jacob's revelation was incomplete because it was before the once-for-all work of the cross and the sending of the Holy Spirit, both of which provide power only dreamed about by Jacob and the nation that came out of his loins. That does not make the example of Jacob's life less important, but it brings the realization that you and I now have far more access to the power of God for change in our lives.

I also want to once again give credit to the book that helped open my eyes to this dysfunction in my life and encourage struggling couples to use it as a tool to begin their own journey. "Living with the Passive-Aggressive Man" by Scott Wetzler was the book that started the educational process that is still going on today. It clearly shows the issues involved in passive-aggressiveness, which Kathy and I needed badly in order to truly understand the issue, but it does not approach it from a spiritual standpoint. That's one of the reasons I decided to put my thoughts and experiences down with the background of a biblical story. Spiritual answers to life's toughest situations are often caught by watching how God worked in the lives of biblical characters. Walking alongside Jacob has confirmed within me the dangers of passive-aggressiveness as well as the truth of a Father God Who is in our lives for the long haul and will do whatever is necessary to show us that His Face is far more beautiful than our little protected universes.

NOTE: I am more than aware that God is not totally male. There are plenty of biblical references to God in feminine terms. So when I refer to God as "Father" or use masculine pronouns in this study, it is in deference to the story that is being used as a blueprint for my thoughts. It may also hint at the need for a passive-aggressive man to grow into a healthy and balanced masculinity.

Thoughts From Kathy

Finding a Way to Talk About It

One of the things that helped Boyd accept the fact that we were dealing with passive-aggressiveness was how I described it to him. Instead of talking about what he was doing and blaming it on him as a person, I would talk about how "the dysfunction" or "the passive-aggressiveness" was affecting us.

People who are justifying their actions sometimes need to see themselves separated from those actions in order to see the negative issues tied to those actions. This is not denial of reality but a non-threatening way to get a person to see reality.

19. DEALING WITH ANGER

As I mentioned while we were at the wrestling arena of Peniel, I need to flesh out the idea of a new identity and how it can be one of the major keys to the healing of a passive-aggressive man. Indeed, what I am about to share is a major key to the transformation of any person who finds himself or herself at the point of desiring true change. And it will take more than one chapter to do it justice.

The first step in discovering the identity given a person by God is the relinquishing of control over that identity. It can be given only by the One Who created it. A person has to forsake his own thoughts about his life, because he realizes they are not God's thoughts, which are far higher than his thoughts (Isaiah 55:7-9) This is especially true for a passive-aggressive man who has created a universe within his own thoughts and has become very comfortable living in that universe. Admitting to the difference between his thoughts and his partner's thoughts or his family member's thoughts or his co-worker's thoughts is a good start, but it's simply not enough. There has to be a radical re-ordering of his mind...a transformation by the renewing of his mind (Romans 12:1-2). He has to understand the power of having a new mind, a new heart, and a new spirit placed inside of him (Hebrews 8:10; Ezekiel 36:26).

Once that understanding is established, he has to take the primary issues that underly his dysfunction and offer them up to be transformed in the fire of God's love. For a passive-aggressive man, those two issues are anger and fear, which lead to deceit and block true intimacy and communication. The truth found in Scripture about these issues has to find its way into his being and become part of his new way of thinking and acting.

James 1:19 tells us to be "**slow to become angry**", but I don't believe that means to store up anger so that it erupts later on. The passage goes on to say that anger "**does not produce the righteousness that God desires**". In Ephesians 4:26, Paul quotes Psalm 4:4, which says, "**In your anger do not sin.**" He goes on to say, "**do not let the sun go down while you are still angry.**" The Psalmist puts it this way: "**Meditate within your heart on your bed, and be still.**"

Perhaps what those inspired writers were trying to say is that we cannot take anger lightly. It has to be managed. As much as he might think differently, a passive-aggressive man does not manage his anger. His anger manages him. One of the things I've learned to do as I've realized this tendency about myself is to stop as soon as I feel anger rising up and ask myself where it started. If Kathy or someone else says or does something that causes anger to rise up in me, I try to reflect on the situation and, when it involves Kathy, even talk through it with her and put words to my feelings. This typically stops the anger of the moment from stewing long enough to find a passive-aggressive outlet.

Another way to put a healthy spin on anger is to watch it modeled by Jesus. The passages that show him expressing anger seem to have a common element. We see Him commanding Satan to get behind Him at the end of his wilderness temptations and again when Peter tried to prevent Him from moving toward the cross. We listen as He verbally scourges the Pharisees for their hypocrisy. We watch him as he curses a fig tree for not bearing fruit, a fig tree that was a symbol of the people of Israel in His day. And, of course, we're often taken back by the fierceness He showed as He cleared out the Temple courts.

So what is the common denominator in these stories? Anger in the life of Jesus was triggered by the dissonance between the truth He had known from before the world was created and the human distortion of that truth.

When He was tempted to stray from becoming the sacrifice for the sins of the world by a voice that promised Him an easier way - the way of a worldly kingdom, His reaction was immediate and forceful - **"Get behind Me, Satan!"** He knew that the slightest turn in the direction of an alternative route would keep Him from bringing into time and space the power of the Lamb slain from the foundation of the world. Even when one of His closest friends suggested a different way, His response was grounded in anger.

The word pictures Jesus used when confronting the Pharisees were filled with anger. I can't imagine Him calling them **"white-washed tombs"** or **"blind guides"** (Matthew 23) with a calm and peaceful voice. He was dealing with a group of men who were teaching the people He had chosen centuries before and loved through their constant rebellion that their God was a spiritual bean-counter Who was more interested in their adherence to every minute detail of His law than in having a loving relationship with the Author of that law.

The fig tree that was the brunt of His anger was a vivid picture to Jesus of how this misdirected leadership had caused the people of Israel to be a fruitless tree. He knew the mission His Father had for this people - a mission to share His unbelievable love with the rest of the world - and He saw how far removed they were from that mission.

Even when He brought a whip into the Temple courts to drive out the moneychangers, it was because He knew that His Father's House was supposed to be a house of prayer instead of the den of thieves that system had allowed it to become.

So...in all of these instances, Jesus spoke or acted in anger because what He saw happening around Him was diametrically opposed to how He knew it was supposed to be.

The anger that motivates a passive-aggressive man is the exact opposite of this. It's brought to the surface not when the truth has been co-opted by a lie but rather when the little universe he has deceived himself into believing as the truth is confronted by the stark reality of the truth itself. This upsetting of a passive-aggressive man's finely-constructed world draws out anger like a moth to a flame. And someone is definitely going to get burned.

A man who is ready to admit to his passive-aggressive tendencies would do well to spend some time meditating on the core of the motivation for anger in the life of Jesus. If he can rewire his thinking to default to the righteous anger that arises in defense of the truth, then his usual unrighteous anger, which arises in defense of himself, will fall by the wayside.

THOUGHTS FROM KATHY

HEALTHY ANGER

Passive-aggressive men don't need to be afraid to speak the truth from an emotional place, because I think most people understand when someone is trying to speak a difficult truth. Boyd has become more comfortable expressing his anger in healthy ways instead of holding it in until it becomes unhealthy.

20. DEALING WITH FEAR

N ow, let's dig a little deeper. I would venture to say that 95% of the anger that slithers into the psyche of a passive-aggressive man comes out from under one of the slimy rocks of fear - the fear of failure, the fear of confrontation, the fear of competition, the fear of intimacy, the fear of self-disclosure, the fear of losing control, and sometimes just plain old fear. If this is true, it is imperative to know the spiritual truth regarding fear.

There are tons of references to fear in Scripture, but we need to emphasize a couple and once again look to the life of Jesus as our example. Of course, there is a healthy fear or awe of God Himself. Although that's not my focus here, I don't want to pass it by without saying that this kind of fear, which recognizes the proper place for God in our lives - on His throne and in control - is foundational to understanding everything we've seen in this study of passive-aggressiveness.

But that is not the fear that underlies the thoughts and actions of a passive-aggressive man.

One of the most powerful verses in the Bible's arsenal against fear is the often-quoted II Timothy 1:7:

"For God has not given us a spirit of fear, but of power and of love and of a sound mind."

In other words, if we are motivated at all by fear, we have to recognize that this motivation is NOT from God.

Another foundational verse regarding fear is I John 4:18:

"There is no fear in love; but perfect love drives out fear, because fear has to do with punishment. The one who fears is not made perfect in love."

The very purpose of God in creating beings who have the capacity to choose Him out of love comes to the forefront here. It is God's intention to keep us free from fear by inviting us into the perfect love of the Trinity that existed even before the world was created. Our picture of God must be switched from a vengeful Judge waiting to be appeased to a loving Father longing for His adopted children to realize who they are. The only way to make that switch is to believe in and hold onto perfect love.

So how did Jesus exemplify this attitude? When tempted by Satan in the wilderness, He could have easily succumbed to fear. He chose to quote truth from the highest Authority He knew, and those **"it is written"**s (Matthew 4 & Luke 4) were the game-changers. Also, in His final hours, Jesus was confronted by the fear of moving forward with His Father's plan, a plan that centered on His death. At His weakest point, He once again defaulted to the wisdom of His loving Father by saying that if the plan couldn't be altered, **"not my will but Yours be done"** (Matthew 26:39 & Luke 22:42).

If a passive-aggressive man can reach outside of himself and recognize that the actual final word in any situation is not his own - but that of the One Who created him, it would go a long way towards putting fear in its place. This is not easy for someone who, even though he would probably not admit it, has always seen himself in the role of ultimate authority. Knowing God as the source of perfect love is the antidote for the poison of fear.

THOUGHTS FROM KATHY

FACING HIS FEARS

T hose of us who are partners of passive-aggressive men need to encourage them to not be afraid to face the things in their past or present that they're having a hard time dealing with. The anger that ends up coming out in an unhealthy way is often the result of fear, so helping the passive-aggressive man face down his fears is one of the best tools to protect yourself from the destructive side of anger.

21. Dealing With Deceit

I mentioned earlier that anger and fear in the world of the passive-aggressive man lead to deceit. By deceit I mean both the act of lying and the oftentimes worse act of manipulation. Let's once again look at some of the many references to deceit in Scripture and how Jesus lived outside of its clutches.

Beginning with the letters carved in stone by the Divine Finger that commanded His people to **"not bear false witness"** (Exodus 20:16), the seriousness of deception in the eyes of God is clear. We have to understand that the capacity for deception does not exist within the three Persons of the Trinity. **"God is not a man, that He should lie."** (Numbers 23:19) Paul tells one of his sons in the faith about **"God, who cannot lie"** (Titus 1:2).

The web of deception that corrupted creation was spun well outside the glorious fellowship among the Father, the Son, and the Holy Spirit from eternity past and into eternity future. The decision to share that fellowship necessitated that those created to share it would have the capacity to refuse it. This refusal took place in both the supernatural and the natural realms as part of the angelic hosts turned their back on their Creator and then provided the rationalization for the first of humanity to follow in their footsteps. Suddenly lies and manipulation multiplied until the creation looked absolutely nothing like its Creator.

The purpose of God since that point has been to restore what has been corrupted. The magnificent work of Jesus on the cross accomplished this completely, but the old continues to try to convince us that this work has not been done. When it comes to lying, Paul gives the perfect prescription:

> **"Do not lie to one another, since you have put off the old man with his deeds, and have put on the new man who is renewed in knowledge according to the image of Him who created him." (Colossians 3:9-10)**

The only way to deal with deception in our lives is to see Who God truly is and then recognize that we have been given the awesome opportunity to live within His life by turning our backs on our old life. This is not the old "work hard to change yourself" system, which is flawed from the beginning because it operates under the power of the old person. You might see some progress in an area of your life if you concentrate on it enough, but the underlying problem will never let go of its grasp on your old person. However, that same problem has no way to latch onto someone who is living as a new person empowered by the pure life of God.

Once again, our best role model is the One Who experienced that pure deceit-free fellowship and then entered into time and space to show us what it looked like. Jesus lived a life untouched by lies and manipulation.

His first recorded words show that He was not bent toward lying or manipulating a situation in His favor. When Joseph and Mary found Him at the Temple confounding the teachers of the Law, He went straight for what He knew was the truth about His purpose in life -

"Why did you seek Me? Did you not know that I must be about My Father's business?" (Luke 2:49)

He didn't turn to excuses or try to make His parents feel guilty for not knowing where He was. He instinctively responded with the highest truth He knew.

This happened time and time again when He was confronted by the Pharisees and teachers of the Law. He never compromised truth in order to be more acceptable to them. In fact, the truth coming from His mouth was often hard for them to swallow. Why did He not want to be accepted by the group of men who were obviously the most righteous of his day? Because their righteousness was of an inferior kind than what He knew was available - what He would die to provide.

One last example would be the conversation between Jesus and Pilate. When Pilate asked if He was the King of the Jews, Jesus answered, **"It is as you say."** (Matthew 27:11; Mark 15:2; Luke 23:3) In John's fuller version, Jesus adds,

> **"You say rightly that I am a king. For this cause I was born, and for this cause I have come into the world, that I should bear witness to the truth. Everyone who is of the truth hears my voice." (John 18:37)**

Jesus once again dialed in the truth of His central purpose.

I'm afraid the typical passive-aggressive man is less like Jesus and more like Pilate, who responded with the famous line, **"What is truth?"** (John 18:38) It's so much easier to allow truth to be elastic enough to fit any situation. At least that's how the passive-aggressive man treats truth. Now, I know that the bigger questions about truth deal with something a bit different than what is true or false in a specific situation. But the underlying principle is still the same. When someone knows the truth about his relationship with God and what purpose his life has because of that relationship, all forms of truth become easier to spot. He has no reason to shift his allegiance to a foundation that changes from one situation to the next. The key is understanding that God is the only One Who has a right to declare what is true.

Once that is done, the next step is to receive the new man that was made available because of the cross of Jesus. That man is the one who is being changed and renewed into the image of the One Who made him. When someone becomes like Jesus, it takes lying and manipulation out of the picture, because his life is no longer tied to the dysfunctions of his past but to the fully-functional glory of the Three in One.

Thoughts From Kathy

Reaching A Place of Trust

It took a period of time for Boyd to show me that he was consistently telling the truth and not manipulating me. As he experienced the process of healing, we had to slowly walk through each situation we encountered until I could reach a place of trust.

22. DEALING WITH INTIMACY

I n Chapter 19, I wrote the following about the primary issues underlying the passive-aggressive dysfunction: "For a passive-aggressive man, those two issues are anger and fear, which lead to deceit and block true intimacy and communication." At the time, I didn't know how insightful that statement was. It very succinctly describes the process I've been talking about throughout the book. So that chapter and each chapter since has taken one of these elements and placed it under the microscope of God's written Word and the blazing light of His living Word.

If the fear that causes unrighteous anger can be cast out by the perfect love of God and that anger can be replaced by the righteous anger that defends the eternal truth of God's purpose, the new person created by God to be like Him will live without deceit. What follows will be the kind of intimacy and communication for which the partner and friends of the passive-aggressive man long.

Jesus reveals the deepest part of His heart in His prayer recorded in John 17. He says in verse 5,

"And now, O Father, glorify Me together with Yourself, with the glory I had with You before the world was."

Verses 22-26 continue the picture of His desire for His followers to experience this same glory:

"And the glory which You gave Me I have given them, that they may be one just as We are one: I in them, and You in Me; that they may be made perfect in one, and that the world may know that You have sent Me, and have loved them as You have loved Me. Father, I desire that they also whom You gave Me may be with Me where I am, that they may behold My glory which You have given Me; for You loved Me before the foundation of the world. O righteous Father! The world has not known You, but I have known You; and these have known that You sent Me. And

I have declared to them Your name, and will declare it, that the love with which You loved Me may be in them, and I in them."

So the goal of God's work in our lives is for us to share the same kind of intimacy and communication with Him and the people He puts in our lives that is shared by the Father, Son, and Holy Spirit. This is impossible for a passive-aggressive man as long as he refuses to deal with the fear, anger, and deceit that build the barrier keeping such intimacy and communication from happening.

The method Jesus chose to transfer that intimacy was two-fold. Instead of teaching a doctrine or a set of commandments or principles, He simply said, **"Follow me."** The people who followed Him got to experience up close and personal what a fearless and deceit-free life of intimacy was like. And they were able to later transfer that intimacy to others by continuing to experience His Presence as they met together. The second part of the method was to provide His very Spirit to make this experience possible.

The sad fact is that this method of intimacy transfer has been hijacked over the years by a totally different kind of method. The church which bears the name of Jesus began as an organic expression of people who were introduced to a risen Messiah Who replaced their old lives with new ones, gave them the power of His Spirit and placed them in intimate community to help them live out those new lives. What it became was just another religion with its rules and rituals.

A passive-aggressive man who truly wants to be free of his dysfunction cannot approach it with the temporary power of religion, because neither legalistic rules nor the call for "more faith" can effect true and lasting change. The only thing that can is the decision to follow the One Who offers radical transformation and the persistence to allow Him to complete that transformation over time through intimate relationship with Him and with others in the same process. But a man hiding in his own little universe will keep this transformation from happening.

I've noticed that there are a ton of passive-aggressive men who have a sincere faith in Jesus and are part of local churches - many of them playing vital roles in their churches. Perhaps this is because the deterioration of the original intent for the church has created an atmosphere where passive-aggressiveness can thrive, an atmosphere not of true intimacy and transparency but of game-playing and superficial relationships. A man searching for a way out of his dysfunction will rarely find help in that world. However, it is necessary for him to find relationships of depth where the mask can be removed and healing encouraged.

It goes without saying that a passive-aggressive man who is in an intimate relationship must find the courage to step as deliberately as possible toward true intimacy with his partner. This may be the most difficult step of the whole process and yet the most rewarding. Those who are in relationship with this kind of man desperately long for the kind of communion and communication that is only possible when he recognizes his passive-aggressiveness and turns his back on it.

As always, the best cue is taken from Jesus Himself. The way Paul describes the relationship Jesus has with His bride is extremely informative. Ephesians 5:25-29 says,

> **"Husbands, love your wives, just as Christ also loved the church and gave Himself for her, that He might sanctify and cleanse her with the washing of water by the word, that He might present her to Himself a glorious church, not having spot or wrinkle or any such thing, but that she should be holy and without blemish. So husbands ought to love their own wives as their own bodies; he who loves his wife loves himself. For no one ever hated his own flesh, but nourishes and cherishes it, just as the Lord does the church."**

The way of Jesus with His bride involves self-sacrifice and deep communication that washes her clean. His focus is on what He can do to make her the glorious and beautiful woman He chose from eternity to be His. He places her need for nourishment and cherishing on the same level as His own desires. Can any person refuse to thrive in the midst of that kind of love?

I know this sounds frightening to a man still in the clutches of the passive-aggressive dysfunction, but the picture of Jesus loving His bride has to be his focus, because it has the most potential power to draw the man out of his junk and into a place of purity beyond the reach of dysfunction. I still find myself meditating on it and grieving over the enormous gulf between its stunningly beautiful vision and the reality of my thoughts, words, and actions.

Final Thoughts From Kathy

There Really is Hope!

T he work of forgiveness and redemption is hard. But I can say that it's definitely worth the struggle it took for us to get to a point of forgiveness – me forgiving Boyd as well as Boyd forgiving me. Our life together wasn't always bad before we found ourselves looking for a book to help us. We had plenty of good moments. But the destructive nature of passive-aggressiveness was taking an awful toll. If you're just now starting out on this journey to healing, don't give up. Boyd and I have spent the last two decades proving the lady in the bookstore wrong. There really is hope!

A Meditation on His Heels

The rabbis in the time of Jesus would lead their disciples around from place to place teaching them. As they traveled, the rabbi would kick up a cloud of dust that would literally cover those following in his footsteps. This is captured in the old rabbinic saying: "May you be covered in the dust of your rabbi."

If we take that picture and bring it into the context of passive-aggressive heel-grabbing, it doesn't take much imagination to see the need to grab those divine Heels as He walks in front of us and allow His ways to become ours. The passive-aggressive man has the choice of continuing to grab the heels of those around him in an attempt to use their energy to control and manipulate the universe of his own creation or to reach for the heels of the Rabbi Who walks ahead of him and leads him into the life he was created to live.

Now, those disciples walking with the physical Jesus actually lacked one thing that we have. The power to put God's plan for each of us in motion was unleashed on the cross. Seeing the feet of Jesus as we walk behind Him and follow His lead is one thing. Gazing at the nails in His feet as He hung on that cross is quite another. The blood that flowed from His feet should remind us of the sacrifice that made it possible for us to be free from the power that our sinful dysfunctions have asserted in our lives. Those heels must be grabbed and held forever, because the blood that stained them is our source.

Recognizing the freeing power of his blood-stained heels should then lead us directly to the last picture of the feet of Jesus, the one where they are being washed and kissed in loving worship by a woman who had experienced His forgiveness. We cannot overlook the power of grabbing the heels of Jesus in an act of adoration and worship. With our knees on the ground, our eyes immediately go to His feet. Let's make sure the dust-covered heels we follow and the blood-stained heels that freed us become the tear-drenched focus of our worship.

A FINAL WORD TO PASSIVE-AGGRESSIVE MEN

I f you are a man who struggles like I have with passive-aggressiveness and you've actually read this far, I commend you. You've taken the all-important first step of recognizing the problem. Now I have one last word for you - repent!

Repentance is not just saying you're sorry and then expecting everything to go on as if nothing has happened. Repentance is a willingness to submit yourself to a process that may take a longer time than you would like. Your partner, family, and friends need to see a track-record of change before they can invest into your life again. Trust can be destroyed in a moment, but it may take years for it to be restored.

At this point, I have to encourage you again that it's only through the healing work of the Spirit of God that passive-aggressiveness or any dysfunction can be overcome. Don't even begin to think you can do it yourself. You can't! But the fact that you've got this book in your hands is proof that the Spirit is working in you even now. Ask the Spirit of God to show you the next step. The things I've written here will hopefully help you in the process, but each step has to be Spirit-designed.

The fear you feel right now causing anger to rise up within you has to be challenged. If you can accept the truth that God is perfect Love and that He has an unbelievable life designed just for you, you will have no need to deceive yourself or anyone else by retreating into your own universe. Come out and breathe the air of the only universe that counts - the one God created. It's a whole lot better than yours, believe me!

A Note to My Children

Tanna and Asher,

Even though some of the things I've shared in this book are embarrassing and I wish hadn't been part of our lives, I truly hope you read what I've written about this destructive dysfunction. First of all, it will help you understand a little better what was going on beneath the surface as you were growing up. I believe that I was a reasonably good father, but I know that my passive-aggressiveness definitely affected both of you (and perhaps still does). There is no question that I loved both of you dearly and desired the best for you, but my inability to deal with my fears of rejection, failure, and confrontation led me to do (or not do) things that have made impressions on your lives.

My word to you now is to deal as honestly and quickly as you can with the dysfunctions that God shows you in your own lives. Many of those dysfunctions you learned from me, and some you learned from Mom. Also, there is no such thing as a perfectly functional family, so you've been in relationships with people who come from homes where they learned some level of dysfunction as well.

If you see some of the signs of passive-aggressiveness that I talk about in this book (or any other dysfunction) in either your-self or your significant other, begin now to deal with those signs. You have the opportunity to benefit from the mistakes I made in order to find wholeness in your relationships or marriages more quickly than I have.

And follow the example of your unbelievably patient and yet persistent mother, who wouldn't settle for anything short of God's healing. Even after working on it for a couple of decades, we're still in the process, but we're seeing more light every day. We pray constantly for both of your families, and we love you enough to speak truth into your lives when the Spirit directs us.

I love you both more than I've ever told you,

Dad

A Note to My Grandchildren

Jaden, Rebekah, James, Ezekiel, Benjamin, Elliana, and Ephraim,

Thankfully, the issues revealed in this book were mostly healed by the time you guys started coming into our lives. But I would guess that you might be curious enough to read it someday, so I wanted to say something specific to you.

If there's one thing I'd like you to take away from reading this book, it would be the importance of dealing with the harmful tendencies in your lives and relationships as soon as you can identify them. Because I did not deal early on with the dysfunction you read about in this book, the first half of my marriage to your grandma was marked by a lot of unnecessary pain and confusion.

Please know that whatever issues arise can find healing from the same source that brought life back to our marriage. Don't look for an overnight miracle, but you can expect an evolution orchestrated by the loving God I talk about in this book.

I hope the transparency with which we wrote this book will be an example of the courage to face tough issues, and I pray it shows that change is truly possible.

All of you have added incredible joy to my life, and I love you deeply.

Grandpa

A Note to My Wife

K athy,

Your love for me has never been more real than when it dug in its heels and forced me to look straight into the ugly face of my sinful dysfunction. I know that I could not have worked through all of this if it were not for God's love, but I also know that I would not have worked through it were it not for your love.

This book has been a kind of therapy for me as I've gone back through the lessons we've learned together, but it's a kind of love letter to you as well. When I finally came back to it after letting it simmer for the past ten years, I had two reactions. First, I was struck again by the depth of my dysfunction you endured for years and had to tell you again how sorry I am. And second, I was elated to look at where our relationship is today. Your love language is not flowery words or even gifts.

You respond best to the practical changes that I allow God to make in my life. I hope this book is not only a clear picture of where we were but also a reminder of how far we've come.

I know that the process is still ongoing, but I'm more assured than ever that I'm surrendering to that process. Even when we have an occasional setback, it doesn't destroy or even discourage me. The healing is far enough along that it now has a life of its own...and the One Who created that life will see that it's not aborted.

You are truly my partner in this life, and I'm proud of the growth I've seen in you. You are more clearly aware of who you are than anyone else I know. I'm very sorry for the things you've had to suffer because of the dysfunction I brought into our relationship. You didn't deserve that suffering, but you've come out on the other side of it more whole than ever. And I pray that both of us have come out on the other side of it more in love with each other than ever. Thank you again for pushing me to the point of change.

You've been my love for more than four decades (working on five),

Boyd

Our Winter Feels Like Spring

During the heart of the COVID pandemic in 2020 and 2021, Kathy and I discovered something wonderful. Because of the changes that took place in our relationship during our two decades of working through what you've read about it this book, we surprised ourselves with how wonderfully we got along during those years when the world seemed to be falling apart around us. We spent a vast majority of our time just the two of us in our home. And we thrived! We were closer than we'd ever been. The passive-aggressiveness that had haunted our marriage rarely raised its ugly head, and when it did, we quickly beat it back down. When we realized how far we'd come, it was an amazing feeling!

On New Year's Eve of 2021, I presented Kathy with a song I had written that spoke to our journey. Now that you've read this book, you'll be able to understand what's behind these lyrics. Maybe one day I'll record the song itself, but for now,

you can read it as a poem to put a little bow on everything
we've tried to say here.

Our spring was full of promise
As our futures merged to one
But if I'm truly honest
A part of me chose to run
And in that early season
I could barely feel your pain
Each mistake a reason
For another drop of rain
And as the summer brought the heat
It burned most everything
Til it seemed
We'd forever lost our spring

With summer came our children
A mix of joy and grief
But, too often hidden,
I gave you small relief
And in that second season
As we grew a world apart
I added to the reasons
That shuttered up your heart
And then the autumn of our lives
Dropped leaves on everything

Til it seemed
We'd forever lost our spring

Now autumn made it clearer
As we named what came between
And every step grew nearer
To the life we'd never seen
And in that dying season
Life peaked out from the grave
I added fewer reasons
And you came out from your cave
But then the snows of winter came
And covered everything
Til it seemed
We'd forever lost our spring

Though winter should be frozen
By the storms of seasons past
That's not the path we've chosen
But instead we chose to last
And in our final season
We hold each other close
And that is now the reason
It's our winter I love most
For though the other seasons came
And tested everything

Now it seems
Our winter feels like spring

About the Authors

Boyd Barrett is a real estate appraiser in Roswell, NM, but spends a great deal of his time bringing creative projects to life, both for himself and others. He is a stage/film/voice actor, author, songwriter, screenwriter, playwright, and an audiobook narrator/producer. You can find out more about Boyd at https://boydbarrett.com.

Kathy Barrett works with Boyd in their appraisal business in Roswell, NM. She fell in love with scrapbooking and card-making about twenty-five years ago and now owns a scrapbooking business called The Scrap Architect. She and Boyd have two children and seven grandchildren. You can find out more about Kathy at https://thescraparchitect.com.